GOD
of My
Father

Other books by Larry Crabb:

Basic Principles of Biblical Counseling

Effective Biblical Counseling

Encouragement: The Key to Caring
(with Dan Allender)

The Marriage Builder: A Blueprint for Couples and
Counselors

How to Become One with Your Mate

Understanding People: Deep Longings for Relationship

Inside Out

Men & Women: Enjoying the Difference

Finding God

GOD
of My
Father

*A Son's Reflections
on His Father's
Walk of Faith*

DR. LARRY CRABB, JR.
& LAWRENCE CRABB, SR.

ZondervanPublishingHouse
Grand Rapids, Michigan

A Division of HarperCollinsPublishers

God of My Father
Copyright © 1994 by Lawrence J. Crabb, Jr., Ph.D., P.A., dba,
Institute of Biblical Counseling, and Lawrence Crabb, Sr.

Requests for information should be addressed to:
 Zondervan Publishing House
 Grand Rapids, Michigan 49530

International trade paperback ISBN 0-310-38617-9

Library of Congress Cataloging-in-Publication Data
Crabb, Lawrence J.
 God of my father: a son's reflections on his father's walk of faith
/ Larry Crabb, Jr. & Lawrence Crabb, Sr.
  p.   cm.
 ISBN 0-310-38610-1
 1. Faith development. 2. Parenting—Religious aspects—
Christianity. 3. Children—Religious life. 4. Crabb, Lawrence J. 5.
Crabb, Lawrence. I. Crabb, Lawrence. II. Title.
 BV4637.C72 1993
 248.8'421—dc20   93-44707
                                                              CIP

All Scripture quotations, unless otherwise noted, are taken from the
Holy Bible, New International Version NIV®. Copyright © 1973,
1978, 1984, by International Bible Society. Used by permission of
Zondervan Publishing House. All rights reserved.

Published in association with Sealy M. Yates, Literary Agent,
Orange, CA.

Edited by Sandra L. Vander Zicht
Interior design by Rachel Hostetter
Jacket design by David Marty Design
Jacket illustration by Michael Ingle

Printed in the United States of America
94 95 96 97 98 / ❖ DH/ 10 9 8 7 6 5 4 3 2 1

This edition is printed on acid-free paper and meets the American
National Standards Institute Z39.48 standard.

To the women who share our story:
Isabel, Rachael, Phoebe, Carolyn, and Kim

CONTENTS

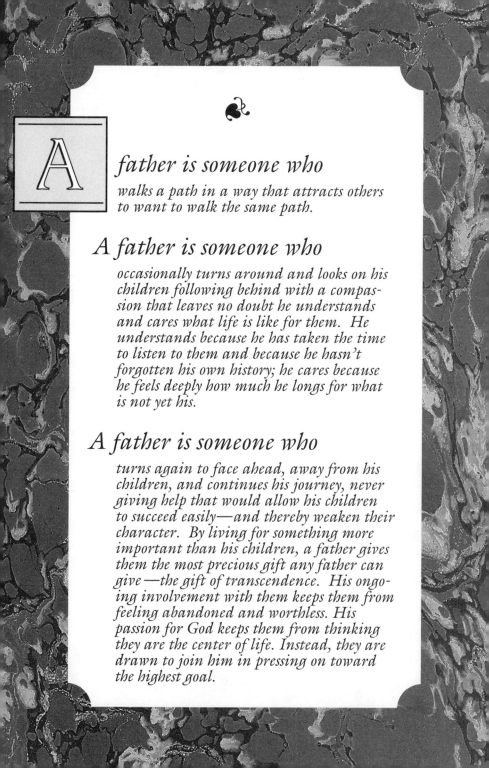

A

father is someone who

walks a path in a way that attracts others to want to walk the same path.

A father is someone who

occasionally turns around and looks on his children following behind with a compassion that leaves no doubt he understands and cares what life is like for them. He understands because he has taken the time to listen to them and because he hasn't forgotten his own history; he cares because he feels deeply how much he longs for what is not yet his.

A father is someone who

turns again to face ahead, away from his children, and continues his journey, never giving help that would allow his children to succeed easily—and thereby weaken their character. By living for something more important than his children, a father gives them the most precious gift any father can give—the gift of transcendence. His ongoing involvement with them keeps them from feeling abandoned and worthless. His passion for God keeps them from thinking they are the center of life. Instead, they are drawn to join him in pressing on toward the highest goal.

Introduction

In the early spring of 1988, during a visit with my parents in their South Carolina home, I noticed a spiral-bound, red notebook lying on the coffee table among the magazines and books intended for decoration and casual reading. Yielding to curiosity, I picked up the notebook.

More than half the pages were covered with my father's handwriting, written with obvious disregard for legibility. With growing eagerness, I flipped through the pages, doing my best to decipher those sentences that began or ended a section. I read sentences like:

- My most severe trial of faith has long been my mother's poverty.
- How I wish I could have known my father!
- I feel that I've made such little contribution. Will I be missed when I die?
- If only I could express what I feel toward my wife and sons.

My curiosity changed to nervous excitement. I felt like a trespasser, entering where I had not been invited.

When Dad returned from his errand, I asked him what the writings were. "Oh, those," he said with a shrug. "When I can't sleep at night, I sometimes get up and write about whatever is going through my mind. Sort of a diary, I guess. I ramble in any direction that seems interesting at the time. It's a bit of a release for me. Maybe it's the prerogative of older people to look over life and say whatever they feel like saying."

"Do you mind if I read through it?" I asked.

"Can't imagine that you'd find much of interest. But sure, read whatever you like."

I found the contents of that notebook more than fascinating. I couldn't put it down. In what I have since dubbed his "midnight ramblings," my father poured out his heart, giving free rein to his mind and imagination, reflecting without censorship on things that mattered deeply to him. Sometimes I laughed; more than once I cried. In a new way, I was coming to know the man who has influenced me more than any other and to understand more clearly why his influence has been so deep. I was hearing his story.

Reading through those midnight ramblings prompted an idea. Was the value in my father's story and how it affected me greater than just its value to me? Could other people find his story useful? Certainly God intends to pass his truth to succeeding generations through one person mentoring another. If I told the story of how my father mentored me, perhaps others might be encouraged to value more deeply the people God has used to influence them. And maybe a few would more vigorously live their own lives in a fashion that would leave a good mark on those who watched.

The idea that began as I read my father's midnight ramblings has taken form in the book you now hold. This book is about mentoring: how an older person influences a younger person for good. This book is not about the *theory* of mentoring; rather it's an illustration of the *process* of mentoring.

This book is personal, more personal than any other book I have written, and more personal, I suspect, than other books about mentoring because my mentor is my father. Not many people have an identifiable mentor. And among those who do, very few would point to their father.

I am in the dwindling minority of people who have been drawn to love God by their fathers. For many people, *father* is a bad word meaning one who abandons, abuses, demeans, and demands perfection. Small wonder that fathers too often represent obstacles, not avenues, to enjoying the idea of God as Father. I hope this book will increase the number of children in the next generation whose fathers *reveal* God to them, rather than distort or obscure him.

I asked Dad to think back on the road he has now walked for more than eighty years, and to tell the story of key incidents that have shaped his character and faith. Much of what you will read has been taken from his midnight ramblings.

My father's story includes poignant moments. As a five-year-old boy, he stood at the foot of his father's bed and watched him die. He suffered a grief so intense that for a brief time it seemed that doubt might overwhelm his faith. As a seventy-eight-year-old man, he reacted to the news of another death—this time his firstborn son— by screaming at God for ten minutes. And later, when it became clear that God wouldn't repent, he held my mother tightly and through their tears they reached a level of intimacy beyond anything they had ever known in more than fifty years of marriage.

Some memories are bittersweet. A coveted football under the Christmas tree replaced the rags bound together by string. But there was no father to shout to the twelve-year-old boy, "Go deep, son! I'll throw you a long one."

Everyone's life is a story whose point is discovered only when that story is lifted up into the larger story of God. After my dad relates one part of his story in each chapter, he reflects on its meaning. He asks, What was God up to when he allowed that to happen? What effect did those events have on me as an honest Christian who has been regularly confronted by a God who makes no sense and who sometimes seems indifferent? As you read his reflections, you will come to appreciate my father's love for the Bible and his intimate familiarity with it. He believes, as I do, that the plot of our larger story, which gives meaning to our lesser tales, is made known only in the book God wrote. Life never reveals its meaning by itself.

As I read each chapter, I pictured myself thirty years behind my father on the same path he walked (with different bumps and detours, of course). I could see myself living out my story, wanting to be more caught up in God's larger story but annoyed that this meant giving up the starring role I so badly wanted.

I then tried to express in words what was happening in my heart as I watched my father still looking back on his life. What goes on inside a person as he feels the impact of his mentor? How am I affected by seeing a faithful man still moving along on a path that I am sorely tempted to abandon?

My father speaks the language of Christianity. His vocabulary, though far richer than mine, is incomplete, often surprising. He says things mature Christians aren't supposed to say, and he says them with an accent not many have, an accent that comes from a world not many people visit.

His passion comes from deep inside him, put there long ago by God and steadily enriched by the Spirit's patient work over many years. His passion grows deeper as it reaches to transcendent heights.

In a talk he gave just before he turned eighty, my father spoke of catching "a whiff of heaven," of hearing laughter and music that made him long to join the party of glorified saints. That phrase, which moved the audience of three hundred people to tears, reflects the attitude of an older man for whom many pleasures—tennis, energetic health, combing hair—are no longer available but who speaks confidently that the best is yet to come. Because he is still pressing on and looking ahead, I have been deeply encouraged. I have seen the path more clearly marked and have been renewed in my determination to keep going.

As you read this book and use the discussion guide (either with a group or by yourself), I hope that you too will be encouraged to walk the path that eventually brings you near enough the land to smell its fragrance and hear its laughter. And may you resolve to walk that path in a way that others are drawn to follow you. May we become a generation of mentors who, like seasoned sailors, can smell land before we see it. 🐚

CHAPTER

1

Hush!
God Is
in It

At the beginning of each chapter, Dad and I will share some photographs from our family albums. Here are my grandparents, Charles and Laura Crabb, with Cecil, Helen, and Dad (Mabel was not born yet), around 1915.

He made known his ways unto Moses, his acts unto the children of Israel.

A Father's Recollections . . .

Our family numbered six in 1917. We had such good times. Papa was about thirty, mother a bit younger. The four children ranged in age from seven to our one-year-old Mabel. I was five, going on six, in case anyone asked.

Papa had a good job. After serving an apprenticeship in England, he worked as a scientific instrument maker. I loved to mouth that phrase, though I didn't have the foggiest notion what it meant.

Papa, to this five-year-old, seemed at least ten feet tall, omnipotent, omniscient. We all waited for his step on the stairs as he came home soon after the clock he had made struck six o'clock. The first hug was always for my mother.

How he loved her.

When I think of Papa, I always see our house on Germantown Avenue in Philadelphia, Pennsylvania. Germantown Avenue (we called it Main Street) was lined with storefronts, topped by two-story apartments. There was John the Barber, Steven the Plumber, Toplis Drugs, Jollies—hats, caps, pants, men's furnishings— and best of all, Haasis, an ice cream parlor and bakery. A Saturday-night *event* was to take a deep glass dish there for a gourmet fillup. It was never quite deep enough for the six of us, but Papa made sure he split it evenly.

Our storefront housed the Germantown Gospel Hall, our place of worship. A curtained plate-glass window displayed a Bible opened to John 3:16. Someone had underlined the words: *"For God so loved the world that he gave his only begotten Son, that whosoever believeth in him should not perish, but have everlasting life."* The building had two front doors; a wide one opening to the Gospel Hall and a narrow one to the hallway and stairs leading to our second- and third-floor home.

Everything happened on the second floor. The front room, long and wide, was divided by a curtain into Papa's workshop on the right and the parlor on the left. The parlor with its stiff, high-backed chairs, a couch, and a small table was used only for company. I remember the many times I sat uncomfortably while the older people talked.

Papa's workshop was different. In his spare time Papa repaired clocks and watches for Philadelphia jewelers. They often gave him work they couldn't handle. My brother Cecil and I loved to brag about the "tough jobs" only our papa could fix. We watched with fascination as Papa peered through his special magnifying glass to make delicate adjustments to all sorts of springs and wheels.

In back of this front room was the sitting room, with a piano and an old foot-powered bellows organ. Alongside the sitting room was our parents' bedroom. The three older children slept on the third floor.

The kitchen took up the whole width of the house. Here we had breakfast, dinner, and supper. The kitchen was modern for 1917. We had a sink with hot and cold water faucets (the water was heated by a tank on top of the coal range), gas lights, and central heat (a cellar coal furnace). We had windows front and back, some with screens to let air flow through—our version of air conditioning.

Papa was into a rather new thing then—electric lighting. One day he decided to wire the Gospel Hall, a major undertaking for a nonprofessional. He began on Monday evening after supper and worked steadily, except for Wednesday-night prayer and Bible reading. Papa was determined to finish in time for the Sunday-morning communion service, even though the last two nights he had a high fever. That didn't stop him, though. He wrapped cold cloths around his head and kept on working. Papa had electric lights operating on Sunday morning, but he never went to the worship service. He was in bed, a victim of the deadly flu epidemic of 1917. He never recovered.

One day that I cannot forget, perhaps about five days later, Mother and I were alone with Papa. A kind neighbor had taken the other children for a walk. Papa was delirious, tossing about with a high fever, his bedclothes wet with perspiration. Mother instructed me, "Lawrence, stay with Papa. I'll be right back with some cool towels. Remember, don't leave the room, not for a moment."

There I sat feeling very important. I was in charge, taking care of my papa.

Moments after Mother left, Papa sat up in bed. He looked straight at me, but I know he didn't see me. He didn't call me by name. "Leave the room, now!" he said.

How was I to obey both Papa and Mother? I ran to the kitchen in a panic. "Papa made me leave the room; he made me."

Behind me came Papa in his nightshirt, running toward the nearest window, anything to cool the fever that was consuming him.

Mother, about half the size of Papa, grabbed for his arms. I fastened onto his legs. Somehow we managed to force him back to bed. Mother always insisted it was a miracle, an answer to prayer. A fall from the second-floor window could have been fatal.

Papa lived only a few more days. Each day the doctor came to see him but only to make him as comfortable as possible. Years later Mother described in her own words what happened. "I was sitting beside the bed. Somehow I knew this was the end, and for the first time I cried in front of you. God was taking my Charlie after giving us so short a time together. He was leaving me a widow with four children. What was I to do? Then Papa looked at me. He recognized me, and I saw all the tenderness again in his eyes. He sat up and put his arms around me. For a moment I thought he was going to get well. Then he said, 'Laura, Laura, don't cry. *Hush, God is in it.*' Then he was gone."

My baby sister, Mabs, wrote of this many years later, a poem she called "We Five," reproduced here in her own handwriting.

A common phrase
We five possess.
A tally bearing
Happiness.

The shadow bears
A light within it.
At death, he said,
"Hush, God is in it."

Mabs.

A five-year-old boy knows nothing of Romans 8:28. To have told me that "All things work together for good" would have been cruel. All I knew was that God, in spite of our prayers, had let my papa die.

Mother had often prayed as she held us close. "Children," she would comfort us, "Papa will get well. You'll see. God answers prayer. He is able."

To me, Papa's last words, "God is in it," meant only one thing: God let my papa die. He was responsible. He could have made Papa well. He chose not to. Didn't he care? Was he indifferent?

Do I, at age eighty, read too much into a little boy's mind? Perhaps. But I remember a vivid experience that happened within a year after Papa was called home.

I was at my friend Manuel's home, an apartment almost identical to ours. Manuel's papa was about the age of mine. We were playing cops and robbers in the kitchen when he said, "Wow. It's almost six o'clock, Larry. Let's go to your house, get your ball and glove, and play catch."

I was having fun. I didn't see why it was so important that we go out of his house now. After all it would be daylight for at least another hour. "No, we gotta go now," said Manuel as he started for the kitchen door. Then we heard his papa trudging up the stairs, a sound so different from my papa's welcome footsteps.

Manuel was terrified. The door flew open, and Manuel went screaming around the kitchen. His papa chased after him with a strap, or was it his belt? "I'll teach you, you little scamp. I'll teach you a lesson you'll never forget." Manuel's mother tried to come between them while I got out of there quickly!

I didn't see Manuel for several days. He never spoke of this incident, as if I hadn't been there.

God took my papa and left this monster. Why?

Now, after a long, slow learning process, I know that Romans 8:28 is not a mere platitude. I know it is true, but not in the empty "praise the Lord" way it is too often presented. Although I still do not understand why God does all that he does, I believe this verse because I know something of God's character. He is unpredictable. He does not always cooperate with my agendas. It has taken me a long time to think of his unpredictability as delightful. Too often, his sovereignty seems more ruthless than benevolent. But I have learned something of Calvary. I hear the agony of the triune God during those dreadful hours when God through his Son's death was reconciling the world to himself. And his own Son cried out to him, "My God, My God, why have you forsaken me?" With indescribable passion Christ too asked why.

Christ alone knew the real horror of being forsaken. My sense of abandonment was an illusion based on a misunderstanding.

Will I ever learn? Not fully, but God has brought me so much closer to himself in the learning process. The good work already begun will continue until the day of Jesus Christ (Phil. 1:6). That day will come. The anticipation of it is truly a "whiff of heaven."

To tell of Papa without telling of his letter of proposal to his beloved Laura nearly a century ago would omit something revealing about the kind of man he was. Even though most people in our generation might regard the letter as not terribly romantic and as stiff, I have the impression that Papa was a man of deep passion. Notice the three XXX's he added after signing his signature. On the next page is the letter in Papa's own handwriting, reproduced from the original.

As I read that letter, my heart bursts: "Papa, I never got to know you. None of us did except Mother." How I long to know that man, and *I will!*

One phrase of Papa's letter always catches my attention: "Until the time that he sees fit to part us." How soon it all ended, but what years they must have been.

This morning I woke at four o'clock with his words "Hush, God is in it" an almost audible reality. As Papa's words faded, a picture emerged in my mind: Mother leaning over to respond to her sick husband. But Papa was gone.

Ever since the Fall, ever since sin came into the world, and death by sin, this agony has touched all of humanity. Yet each sorrow is uniquely personal and, in a sense, is self-centered. The depths in each of us cannot be shared. I recognize the truth of Proverbs 27:19, "As in water face answereth to face, so the heart of man to man" (KJV).

Yet profound sorrow is so much more than a reflection. Sorrow can mercilessly tear apart the very foundations that years of trust were required to build. "In all their affliction he was afflicted" (Isa. 63:9). Can we grasp the wonder of this? We must! Only One who is totally "other" can fully become one with us when the despair of loneliness becomes overwhelming. How eloquent was that solitary figure on the middle cross as he was reviled by criminals on either side. Listen to his words: "Behold, and see if there be any sorrow like unto my sorrow" (Lam. 1:12 KJV).

18/3/09

1231 Dundas St
Toronto

My dear Laura

Since I suggested & half promised to write to you, I here-with take pleasure in availing myself of this privilege. This letter has reference to our conversation of last Sunday night. When you asked me whether I loved you, you noticed I did not express myself very clearly. It was not because I had doubts in this direction, but because,— being such a new experience, I suppose I did not like to reply. If I am not in love with you Laura, I guess I never shall be. I am not emotional, but my offer to you of Sunday, was not made on the spur of the moment. My feelings & love to you, amply warranted our conversation of Sunday, & I am glad I spoke as regards the next step, which will make so much difference to both of us,— the time depends on circumstances. You know all about my circumstances, & although I would not in any way wish to unduly postpone that day, we must of course be prepared first. I so often feel that I am not worthy of the affection of a Christian woman like yourself, yet I sincerely believe its God that has brought us together. Until the time that He sees fit to part us, I will try, Him helping me, to be all I should be to you. It gives me great joy writing this letter, as I know you understand me, & although you never definately answered my question, I believe the answer has already been shewn me. Until this impression is corrected I shall be happy, as the more I am in your company, the more I seem to want to be. Dear Laura, I have just risen from my knees, having made this letter a matter of prayer. As I believe we can both acknowledge Him in this matter, so I pray & trust that all our lives we may be enabled by His grace, to live to the glory of Him Who love us, & gave Himself for us. I shall of course be very happy to have an answer to this letter, although a verbal answer, if more convenient to you, will be equally acceptable. That you may be happy when you receive this, & that your answer to it may keep me happy is the earnest wish of

Yours very sincerly
Charlie xxx

The verse that begins this chapter reminds us that "He made known his *ways* unto Moses, his *acts* unto the children of Israel." Both in the unspeakable horror of Calvary and in the anguish that so often is ours, God works out his ways. Moses implored, "Show me thy ways." I know, in all that happens, that God has a master plan.

The people of Israel were interested only in his acts—sometimes enjoyable (water from a rock, crossing of the Red Sea), sometimes painful (judgment on worship of the golden calf, forty years of wandering). The older I get, the more I long to see beyond his doings and grasp something of his good plan, his ways.

In this life, we will never have full knowledge of his ways, *but we do know enough of his character to rest.* He has spoken in no uncertain terms. "He that spared not his own Son, but delivered him up for us all, how shall he not with him also freely give us all things?" (Rom. 8:32 KJV). He knows. He truly knows our constant perplexity, and his provision now is an invitation to relax in his love, to hear the sound of his footsteps on the stairs, and to beam with anticipation. There is no whip in his hands. "Trust in him at all times . . . pour out your heart before him: God is a refuge for us" (Ps. 62:8 KJV).

We matter to him. God only knows why. I matter to him, and I mattered to him that night when he let my father die.

A Son's Reflections . . .

Was my grandfather's faith that God was in everything naïve? After all, he died when he was only thirty, before life had enough opportunity to disillusion him. He never lived to be my age. For me, the years from age thirty to age forty-nine have raised questions simple answers can't handle.

He never lived to see his older son, my uncle, remain so long unmoved by the gospel. He never lived to see his grandchildren experience family conflict, job problems, and health scares. He never knew how relentlessly life plays with our emotions, for a time lifting us to heights of joy, then plunging us into the abyss of pain.

I wonder if he looked at life the way younger people typically do, with a naïve optimism that eventually everything works out well. Life may throw you for a few tumbles, but you will always land on your feet. His faith was never tested by the trials that more years bring and never by the struggle of old age.

His dying words, "Hush, God is in it," made no sense to his five-year-old son. God's unpredictability was anything but delightful to him. But now, those words bring enormous comfort to that same boy, over seventy-five years later. And they helped sustain my grandmother during fifty lonely years of widowhood.

Just before my grandmother died, her heart failed and she was unable to speak. Yet somehow, she mustered her last bit of strength and gasped one word that Aunt Mabel could hear: "Hush." Her husband's dying words remained with her through all those years and were on her lips as she went to be with him.

But why? Why do those words have power? Why have they meant so much to his family? Do they really believe it was good that my grandfather died when he did or that out of his death came good that could have come no other way? Is it wrong to wonder if he might have exerted a more powerful influence on his family by living, by developing a more mature faith through more years of blessing and trial, a faith that could then have been passed on to others? Maybe his dying words served the same function as flowers at a funeral: perhaps they hid something ugly under an attractive cover.

Ever since I first heard my father tell the story of his father's death, I've wanted to find comfort in it. But, like so many other stories that should deepen faith, this one doesn't always penetrate to the troubled parts deep within me. Telling someone who wants protection from tragedy that tragedy will come but it's okay because God will be in it does not always promote rest. Yet my father claims that we know enough of God's character to rest.

The severest test to my faith in my forty-nine years has been the long-fought realization that God does not give me the guarantees I want. I want to *know* that my two sons will grow in faith, marry well, live decently, work meaningfully, and give me grandchildren I can enjoy. I want to *know* that my marriage will continue on toward richer levels of intimacy, that health and money will be sufficient to provide for Rachael and me pleasures that only health and money can provide. I want to *know* that my ministry is making a lasting difference for good in people's lives, that my work is worthy of respect, that my critics will admit their error, that the Christian community will continue to enroll in my classes, attend my seminars, and buy my books. I don't want God merely to be *in* tragedy; I want him to *prevent* it.

As I read what I've just written, I feel as if I'm standing knee deep in muck, the muck of arrogant disbelief and demand that are the substance of my diseased heart. Something dark within me, something angry and powerful, expects to be given a formula that if followed will reliably bring about the good I want. I think God owes me this formula. It's my due. Is there nothing I can do to persuade God to protect me from what I fear and give me what I want?

A sense of dread from which I cannot escape arises within me: there are no guarantees. Tragedy might enter my life in any form. How can I hush, knowing only that God will be in whatever happens?

Then I consider the alternative. Suppose God *had* promised to prevent tragedy in the lives of people who trust him. Some people think he has, and they promote a faith that has all the backbone of a worm.

I can more easily watch inane soap operas and irritating talk shows than the television preachers who describe God as a shopping mall filled with every imaginable delight and faith as a credit card with no ceiling and accepted by every store. That message is a lie. It highlights blessings but fails to call us to battle. It teaches recovery from misery, never endurance through hardship. It appeals to the self-centered passion within me for blessings now, the ones I want, on my terms. It reduces our Lord to a clerk who will cheerfully give me whatever I sign for on my credit card. It glorifies the muck God condemns.

If people who teach this are not the frauds I think they are, then Grandfather was a man of inadequate faith; Grandmother too. Had they believed, he would have lived to a ripe old age surrounded by all the good things of life. Grandmother would never have struggled financially, and their children would all have enjoyed the material, relational, and spiritual success that godly parents want for their kids.

As I look at the alternative to believing that a good God is in the tragedies of life, I find myself returning to my grandfather's faith. I feel a rock beneath my feet. A thirty-year-old man strengthening his family with words of trust is more compelling than all the empty promises of today's false prophets. Resting in the middle of tragedy because God is in it better fits what I know of the Bible and life than covering my fear of tomorrow by trusting God to supply the blessings I want.

Perhaps the promises God has made really are superior to the ones we wish he had made. Maybe things are working together for good in ways that only faith in a better land can grasp. I'm seeing more clearly that my grandfather's faith was not naïve; it has survived the test of years—in my father. 🙠

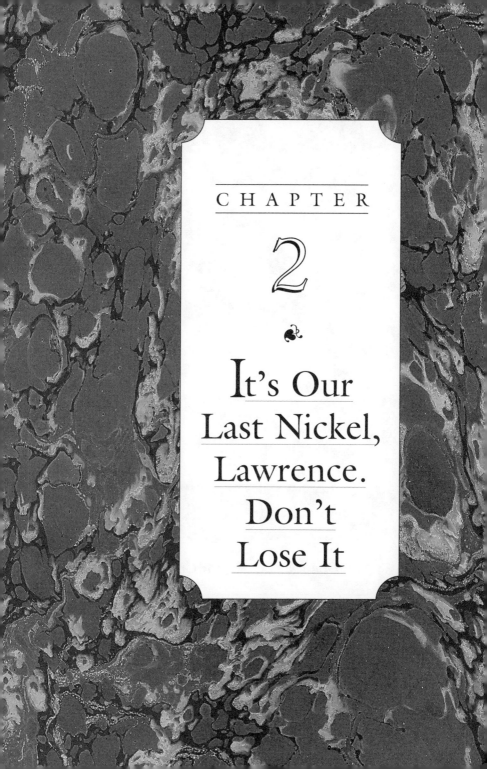

CHAPTER

2

It's Our
Last Nickel,
Lawrence.
Don't
Lose It

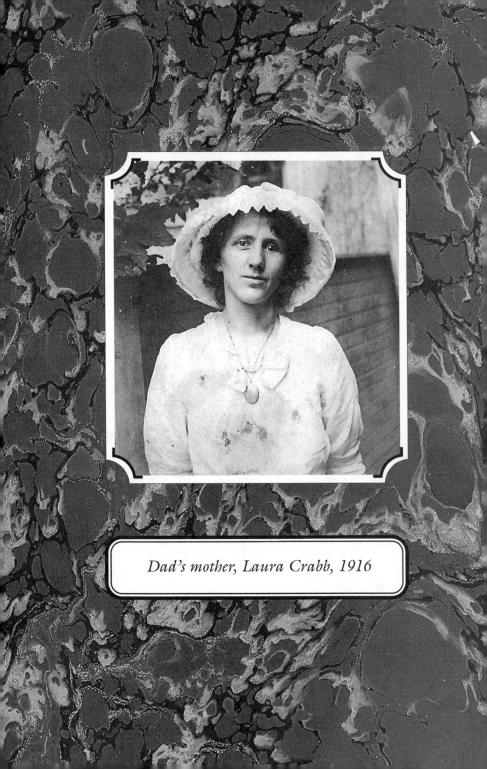

Dad's mother, Laura Crabb, 1916

*And all that believed were
together, and had all things in
common.*

ACTS 2:44 KJV

❦

A Father's Recollections . . .

It was September, 1918. Papa had been dead about
a year. We were still living on Germantown Avenue
in Philadelphia. The kitchen was as it always had
been: the big table with six chairs, the clock Papa had
made still ticking away. But now six o'clock had no special meaning. No footsteps on the stair as Papa came
home.

Nothing had changed. Everything had changed.

One day, I was home alone with Mother.
"Lawrence," she said, "we need a loaf of bread. Will you
go down to the corner for me?" She put a coin into my
hand, coiling my fingers tightly around it. "It's our last
nickel, Lawrence. Don't lose it."

We were truly hard up; it was literally our last nickel. But the word that now stands out as she pressed my
fingers around the nickel was not *last,* but *our.*

Our last nickel. Papa, the head of our home, was
gone, but the oneness remained. What little we had was
shared. It was *ours.*

The following year, when I was seven and my brother, Cecil, was nine, we found after-school jobs in a Mom & Pop fruit store, long before the current child-labor laws. At the end of each day's work we were paid, sometimes only in fruit and vegetables; but whatever it was went to Mother. When we weren't needed at the store, we sold handmade brushes and mops door-to-door. Mother had found a neighbor who made them and let us sell them on consignment. Now and then we made up to a dollar between us. This too went to Mother.

For another source of income, Mother rented out the third floor of our apartment—two rooms that we three older children had used as bedrooms, heated by a kerosene stove—to a widow with two teenage daughters. Now we shared our kitchen and bathroom with three other women. How we managed with such limited facilities, scheduling meal times and Saturday-night baths, is mercifully forgotten.

Mother gave thanks, as always. "Children, you see how God has provided this extra income just in the nick of time." Mother was always conscious of God's care, often quoting from Psalm 68:5, "A father of the fatherless, and a judge of the widows, is God in his holy habitation" (KJV). With her Bible open, she would point to that verse, "There it is, children. God said it."

Mother taught us to pray, not as a group but individually. My prayer each night, kneeling by my bed, went something like this. "Heavenly Father, thou hast taken Papa to be with thyself, and in thy holy Word thou hast promised to take care of mother, brother, sisters, and myself. When I say or do anything to grieve thee, may I quickly confess to thee and so keep happy and smiling for thee. Amen."

Aunt Lily, my mother's sister, contributed much to our home. I know now some of the many ways she helped us, but she never called attention to her giving. She was an English nanny. She must have been a good one because she was placed in full charge of the nurseries of several wealthy families.

On one occasion my sister Helen and I visited Aunt Lily in a palatial home where she had two children under her care, an eight-year-old boy and his six-year-old sister. We had never seen anything like it—games, toys, clothes. The boy had his own pony, which he proudly told us no one else could ride. His sister lost no time in telling us that she would have her very own pony when she was eight. Were we envious? Of course! What kid wouldn't be?

When it was time for us to leave, around six o'clock, Aunt Lily told us to wait a few minutes while she took her children (she called them "her" children) to visit their parents. To my sister Helen and me, this was something totally new. Did this happen every night, or was it a special occasion? What happened on these visits? Of course we didn't ask Aunt Lily such questions at the time, but she must have noticed our faces. Some days later, when she was with us at our home, she explained.

"You see, children, not every home is like yours. The home you visited is almost like two homes. One is the nursery, where I am with the children. The other is where the children's daddy and mother live. They love their children and will do anything for them, but the parents are important, busy people and just don't have time to be with their children as often as they would like. But I take the children to see them almost every night, and they do have good times together."

Good times together! *Almost* every night?

Even to a child, the contrast was only too obvious. For us bedtime was a fun time. Mother would tell stories and read to us, often from Charles Dickens, Papa's favorite author. We would go over the important happenings of the day, display bruises, argue—so many things. And then it was prayer time. Mother never skipped talking with God.

During those growing-up years, Aunt Lily's eyesight had failed to such an extent that she entered a home for the blind in West Philadelphia. One night some workmen carelessly neglected to re-erect a guard rail they had torn down in order to repair a porch directly off her third-floor room. Aunt Lily, not seeing where she was going, fell to her death. The comment of a rescue worker still lingers in my mind: "Such a little thing, so tiny and light."

One tabloid, those vile rags that still pollute newsstands, reported, "Poor elderly lady jumped to her death." What nonsense! She didn't jump; she fell.

Even then I remember thinking, "It wasn't Aunt Lily the rescue worker picked up; it was only a body." She was far away getting her first look at the One who meant so much to her. I really believed she was better off. My father's last words and my mother's simple faith had borne fruit in my life—I knew there was a heaven.

As I write this, it is about four o'clock in the morning. I have just been awakened by the words "sheer delight" as if someone had been yelling them in my ear.

The blankets were too warm, the mattress too comfortable to get out of bed. I lay there wondering what had triggered the phrase "sheer delight."

Then in the delicious fogginess of half-sleep, I was again twelve years old. It was Christmas morning at 4966 Baynton Street, a home we had moved to in 1924, a home that Aunt Lily had helped us to purchase by making the down payment. I was in the parlor, looking at the Christmas tree, seeing but one wonderful present under it—a new football. It was nothing like today's sleek products—just a kit consisting of an outer imitation leather cover, a bladder, needle, lacing, and hand pump. The finished product was overly fat and lumpy, but it sure beat the stuffed piece of cloth Mother had so carefully made up each season. No, this football was the real thing.

That morning as I looked at the tree, I had no thoughts of Mother, up at dawn, trimming the tree my brother and I had picked up free at midnight, beneficiaries of a Philadelphia ruling that vendors must have all trees off the streets by twelve o'clock. She had been laying out gifts, which meant she had gone without so many things she would have liked.

"Sheer delight," a present for me, a present I had been hinting at for many days. Then I thought only of myself, but now looking back over a half-century, I think less of myself and more of Mother standing there beaming. "Sheer delight," the joy of seeing her children enjoying Christmas morning.

"Sheer delight," the joy our Lord experiences as he anticipates the day we will see him face-to-face. In the interim we will have "last nickel" experiences, but soon we will see the "new football," the beginning of his announced intention: "Behold, I make all things new" (Rev. 21:5 KJV). We talk so warmly of *our* glorious future. God knows we have warrant; but perhaps it would be more fitting to think of God's sheer delight as expressed in Proverbs 8:31: "My delights were with the sons of men" (KJV).

A Son's Reflections . . .

Three things stand out to me as I read Dad's words. The first is that I've never sold brushes and mops door-to-door. I have the strangest notion that I've missed out on something. Hardship draws out of us something good and strong and noble, qualities that sometimes develop in no other way.

Second is the phrase "We five." It sounds rich. Nothing bonds us together quite like shared trouble. And nothing speaks more eloquently of the awfulness of the Fall than the fact that it often takes troubles to draw us into deeper unity and dependence on Christ. Of course it sometimes works quite the other way. Troubles divide rather than unite us when they provoke grumbling and fear rather than dependence.

I hate problems. Troubles can function like thick clouds, blocking the sun. Just this morning as we drove to church, my wife, Rachael, told me some news about one of our sons. It was just a passing comment, but it suggested that he might not be doing so well. The comment disturbed me to the point that I lost perspective. A heavy gloom swept through me. I could neither sing the hymns nor listen to the sermon. It took every ounce of spiritual energy I could muster to face what the bad news had aroused in me. I had to face the pride beneath my lost perspective: "I shouldn't have to be troubled by bad news about people I love. My children should always be a source of joy for me. After all, I've worked hard to be a good father."

All of my efforts to regain perspective would have been entirely useless had God not gone to work in the Sunday school class that followed the service. Uncharacteristically, our teacher asked us to pair up at the end of class to pray for one another. The man on my left, whom I had not met before, expressed a personal concern that was identical to the one plaguing me. As I prayed for him, I felt hope returning. The cloud cover broke, and I felt the warmth of God's light. Shared trials drew us together in Christ. What a day awaits us when we'll no longer need problems to encourage trust.

The third thing that stood out was my dad's prayer:

"Heavenly Father, thou hast taken Papa to be with thyself, and in thy holy Word thou hast promised to take care of mother, brother, sisters, and myself. When I say or do anything to grieve thee, may I quickly confess to thee and so keep happy and smiling for thee. Amen."

Is that really how he prayed as a young boy? Did he actually use all that King James English? Today we think of that phrasing with amused condescension and tolerance. Perhaps we're missing something. For him, even today, formal prayer language reflects the appropriate posture of a child kneeling before majesty, a majesty perfectly compatible with intimacy but never blurred by it.

If I have the opportunity and strength to speak when my father goes home to the Lord, I will express gratitude for learning from him the meaning of the word *transcendent:* beyond my life exists a story that is bigger than mine. We live in a very real world, where some children sell mops, others play Nintendo; some families draw together in the middle of hardships, others divide; some children repeat the Lord's name with awe as they pray, others use the Lord's name when they're angry or surprised. But this very real world amounts to nothing more than shadowlands (C. S. Lewis's memorable phrase), a mere vapor compared to the eternal substance of the land where my grandparents and brother now live.

I recall watching my father pray when I was four years old. It was Sunday morning, and about fifty people gathered in a circle to partake of the Lord's Supper. The elements, covered simply with a white cloth, were on a table in the middle. The arrangement was intentional: it spoke of Christ as the center of our thoughts.

Dad stood to pray. I was lying on the floor, looking up at him. Even now, the memory is clear. I thought to myself, *He actually thinks he's talking to Someone. And whoever it is means more to him than anyone else does.*

I've received no greater gift from both my parents than the realization that I was not then and am not now the most important person in their life. Neither was my brother and neither are they to each other (although each runs a close second). Love for family becomes healthy only when it is less consuming than love for God. Only when we love God more than family do we help free our spouses and sons and daughters to become preoccupied with Someone greater than themselves.

We're not the point; none of us. God is. There is a story bigger than ours, a story that transcends every other. And until we see our story as only a subplot in that eternal drama, we'll never see its meaning. I learned that lesson from my father. 🙢

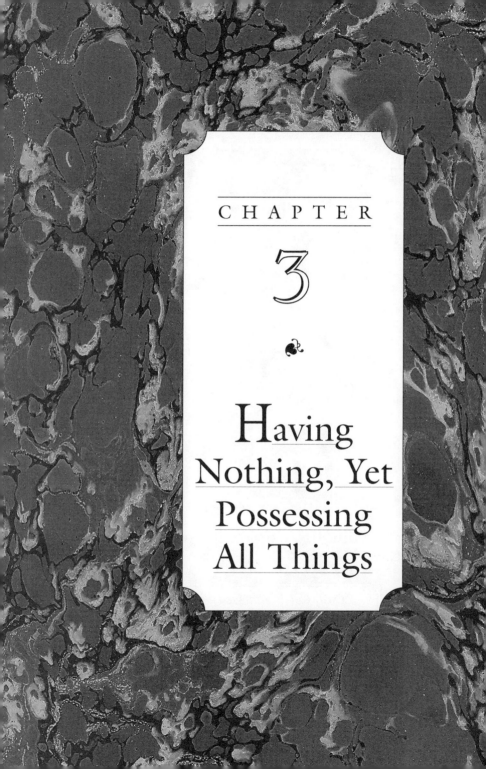

3

Having Nothing, Yet Possessing All Things

Dad, Cecil, and Helen in the backyard of 4938 Germantown Avenue, Philadelphia, about 1917

I have been reminded of your sincere faith which first lived in your . . . mother.

A Father's Recollections . . .

When I was about eight, we moved to a three-story single house on Haines Street, a vast improvement over the storefront apartment of Germantown Avenue. Now we were in a residential neighborhood, homes all around us with one exception. A high wooden fence and a narrow side yard on the left side of our house separated our house from the Harmer Grammar School.

Every morning my brother and I climbed the high wooden fence to go to school. Helen never could get her skirts arranged to follow us. Besides, Mother said it was unladylike for a girl her age to climb a fence. She walked the long way around, almost five minutes, while Mabel, our youngest, watched the daring acrobatics of her two big brothers.

We had no front yard, just three stone steps to the pavement, but we had a huge backyard, narrow and perhaps fifty feet long. Our home was modern by 1920 standards, with electric lights in each room, a full bathroom, and a kitchen with modern appliances. A coal furnace in the cellar provided central heating.

Aunt Lily helped us with the rent, and Mother found a boarder, Mrs. Bell, for the second-floor front room—the *best* room. Mrs. Bell didn't ask for the room; she *demanded* it. Mother often carried meals to her as she lay comfortably in bed. "My health is very delicate, and I do need my rest." She constantly complained of "those noisy children," and sometimes lectured us on our neglect of Bible reading and prayer.

One day Mrs. Bell "bullied" me into confessing Christianity. "Lawrence dear, *you* are a good boy, *you* really are. But *you* know, Lawrence, the Bible says *you* must give an account of every idle word *you* speak." She had a way of verbally underlining *you* as an accusation. "Lawrence, *you* are a sinner. *You* must confess and ask forgiveness. Now!"

She went on for some time, but I was way ahead of her. A lifetime of exposure to Scripture had given me all the correct answers. Finally she was satisfied. "Hallelujah! Lawrence, call your mother. The prodigal has returned."

Following my sweetly coerced profession, the woman insisted that *Mother* buy ice cream and cake so that we might fittingly celebrate my entrance into eternal life. What a party we had, although I suspect there was little joy in heaven over this sinner repenting, the joy our Lord spoke of in Luke 15:10. My own joy was more a response to ice cream and cake than to repentance.

Within a few hours I knew my confession was more exciting than real. A child is certainly capable of coming to know the Savior, but I learned from experience how easy it is to put words into a child's mouth.

Did the sham of this merry making affect my coming to Christ? I've never been sure. If you ask me to give a specific moment, a definite date when I passed from death into life, I confess I cannot do so. Many people can, and I enjoy hearing them tell of a unique conversion experience.

How delightfully unpredictable God is as he goes about seeking and saving the lost! To read of Paul's dramatic about-face on the Damascus road, of the Philippian jailer's agitated cry, "What must I do to be saved" is to enter the very heart of God.

If someone pressed me to pinpoint when I was converted, I can only say, "Possibly when I was twelve." That's when then I first met Harold Harper, a quiet but passionate evangelist whom God brought into my life. This warm-hearted man became a mentor to me, radiating the love of God and the yearning of our Savior for the lost.

He traveled throughout the East, holding meetings in gospel halls or in huge tents with sawdust floors and folding chairs. After he introduced himself and asked my name, his very next words were, "Larry do you know the Savior as *your* Savior?"

"Sure, Mr. Harper, I always have. I pray, I read the Bible, all those things. My papa's in heaven. He was a Christian. And my mother, she's over there, is a Christian too." As usual I had all the right answers.

Mr. Harper smiled, "Larry I have so much to tell you about the One who loves you and died for you, who wants you to know him and care for him as he knows and cares for you." He didn't bully me. He didn't shout, "Hallelujah!" I remember little more of that conversation except that Mr. Harper cared. He took my address and wrote me more about this man, Jesus, who meant so much to him.

Again, I can't give an exact date when I passed from death to life, but I do know that I meaningfully turned to Christ through Harold Harper's encouragement during those adolescent days.

Whether or not I can point to the exact moment of saving faith, the admonition applies, "Forgetting those things which are behind, and reaching forth unto those things which are before, I press toward the mark for the high calling of God in Christ Jesus" (Phil. 3:13–14 KJV).

When I think of Mother, I think more of pressing on than reciting creeds. She continued on through hardships and blessings, believing that no matter what happened, God was in it.

It was while we lived on Haines Street that God, as Mother put it, "went into action." My little sister was accepted into Ellis College, a first-class girls' school in Newtown Square, a suburb of Philadelphia. Within a few months my brother, Cecil, was admitted to the well-known Stony Brook School for Boys in Long Island, New York. Two single women paid all the expenses for these schools in memory of a nephew who had died in an accident.

Both schools offered a scale of living far beyond our experience. In one of his first letters Cecil wrote, "Today at dinner we ate bananas with a fork." I tried it soon after and thought it rather stupid. I did enjoy a snobbish pleasure telling friends about the posh school my brother attended in Long Island. Just the words "Long Island" had a lofty ring, well worth repeating. How tiresome it must have been for our neighbors to be constantly reminded that the Crabbs had a girl in Ellis College and a boy in the Stony Brook School.

Both Mabel and Cecil came home for summer vacations, but to have them taken care of for nine months lifted the financial load on Mother. Helen and I were jealous, but I feel now that we grew into a closeness that we otherwise might never have known.

Our stay on East Haines Street came to an end when Aunt Lily made a down payment on a small row house on Baynton Street, still in Germantown. It wasn't much, a two-story with two rooms on each floor plus a shed kitchen, but it had a coal range for cooking and heating, and hot and cold running water. We had no inside toilet, but this was home. We owned it, and Mother loved it.

This was the house in which we grew up. My sister Helen and I attended the local grammar school, a three-story building with three classrooms on each level. Here the awesome Dr. Parker reigned. We neither liked nor disliked Dr. Parker, but we respected him. When the bell rang for class, those who dawdled often felt the painful flick of his switch. No one was ever injured, but I doubt if Dr. Parker would have much patience with today's indulgent educators.

In those days boys and girls shared classes but were separated at recess by a rail fence. My best friend, Clancy, and I would play catch by this fence to the heart-stirring admiration (so we fondly imagined) of two girls we had selected as worthy. What amazing one-handed catches we made, what bullet-like throws, all with carefully feigned indifference to our audience. We were like a couple of strutting peacocks in full feather. Today, beyond the certainty that one of those girls was named Hazel, I can remember only that they were *so* pretty.

Those carefree days of childhood, were they really that good? The rose-colored glasses of elapsed time obscure our recollections of the actual tensions and anxieties. As I ponder those days, I confess I longed to be part of one of the inner rings: the successful athletes; the boys who made a hit with the girls; the kids who were tough; the people who always had money in their pockets; the kids who were friends with the "right" people.

One of the "right" people was Johnny Rennick, about five feet tall, powerfully built, slick black hair brushed straight back. We called it a "teddy bear," but never to Johnny's face. Johnny was tough! He could lick any kid in the neighborhood. Johnny had a sullen look that intimidated the boys and attracted the girls.

Johnny was at the very center of the "inner ring."

One day, however, I backed Johnny down. Sure, I brag, but this actually happened. Indulge me.

Clancy and I were in business. We shared an afternoon paper route of four hundred customers for the *Philadelphia Evening Bulletin,* which provided us with an express wagon. We were on our way home, when Johnny strutted up to us and sat in our wagon. "Take me down to Logan Street. I'm in a hurry," he barked at us. For a few bitter moments I did just that. I was Johnny's horse, pulling the wagon with Clancy walking obediently beside me.

Then I whispered to Clancy, "Maybe Johnny can lick you, maybe he can lick me, but can he lick both of us together?"

Clancy looked surprised and pleased. "How 'bout that? Tell Johnny to get lost."

I wanted to say to Clancy, "How about you doing the telling, buddy?" but that wouldn't be tough, so I stopped, scared to death. Clancy was backing me up, from a rapidly increasing distance.

"Johnny! Clancy and me ain't pulling you no more. Want to make something of it?" Was this me talking to Johnny Rennick? I stood with shoulders back, fists clenched. When would Johnny tear into me?

Nothing happened.

Johnny got up slowly and gave the wagon a ferocious kick. "Couple of wise guys, huh? I'll get you later. I'd rather walk anyway. Keep your old wagon." The swagger was still there as he walked away, but Johnny was washed up.

Clancy and I stood with our mouths open, hardly believing what we had just seen. "Nothing to it," crowed Clancy. "I told you all *we* had to do was to call his bluff."

Do all Johnnys chicken out so easily? I doubt if I have the guts to assemble statistics.

This was growing up on Baynton Street—Mrs. Bell, Harold Harper, Johnny Rennick, and inner rings. But somehow in it all was Mother's unrelenting faith that even though her husband had died, God was in everything.

Premature and tragic from our perspective, my father's death was the choice of an inscrutable God. To speak of God's unexplained and unpredictable choices as delightful requires a faith that sees beyond his *deeds* to his *ways*, into his character, which he longs to reveal.

As I look back, I know that Mother grasped the full import of her husband's last words. Mother wrested comfort from the most impossible circumstances. Like

Jacob, she wrestled with God and prevailed. She echoed Jacob's cry, "I will not let thee go, except thou bless me" (Gen. 32:26 KJV).

For her "God is in it" was more than a platitude. Mother was never guilty of dramatic pseudo-spirituality. Her faith was not the breezy spirit of the shallow, but the joyful confidence of one who knows God. We children rarely knew the strain she was under in providing for us: clothes, school necessities, and food. We never knew what it was to be other than well fed.

We loved her, but we loved her in the same way we often love God, sadly indifferent to his longing for intimate relationship, coming to him only as need dictates. With Mother, it was "Please sew this button back on." Or "Can you fix this rip in my jacket?" Or, "Where are my sneakers?" Did she sometimes long for a hug and a, "Mom, you're really something!" Of course she did.

Even though Mother has been dead for many years, she is alive in a bliss we can only imagine, enjoying things she never had on earth. Her faith and joy during her life prove the emptiness of the prosperity gospel so popular today. Who better than Mother earned the freedom from care so glibly promised by self-serving proclaimers of material reward in the here and now? God alone knows why some people are so blessed in the things of this life while others lack. To equate prosperity with piety is a cruel lie.

Who can look at Jesus, the man of sorrows who was acquainted with grief, and not be appalled by those who say that the godly will always be blessed with the comforts of life. What does it mean that he will withhold "no good thing . . . from them that walk uprightly" (Ps. 84:11 KJV)? Can it be that our definition of "good thing" is in error? Mother knew far better than most the "peace of God, which passeth all understanding" (Phil. 4:7 KJV). That is true prosperity, and now she enjoys unrestrained blessing that I soon will share.

Mother's life fleshed out the words from 2 Corinthians 6:10: "As poor, yet making many rich; as having nothing, and yet possessing all things" (KJV). Perhaps now I better grasp the truth that God is indeed the defender of widows.

Papa was right. God was in it.

❧

A Son's Reflections . . .

As I read Dad's report of life on Baynton Street, I think of an innocent joy that neither he nor I have known since our childhoods, a joy in which tomorrow meant only more fun.

One of my most vivid memories is Christmas morning forty-two years ago. I was seven. My self-appointed task was to rouse the family with the noise of a badly but powerfully blown bugle. It was time for fire in the fireplace; Bing Crosby's "White Christmas" on the record player; Mother's sausage-filled, syrup-drenched popovers on the breakfast table; the presents piled high beneath the tree, waiting to be ripped open.

My brother, Bill, did not respond appreciatively to the bugle blast in his ear. Mother and Dad received it more graciously. Dad started the fire, Mother turned on the oven, and I carefully laid Bing on the turntable. Everything was as it should be: Eden's bliss recovered. Even Bill's grumpiness disappeared.

The four of us could have posed for a Norman Rockwell painting. Life was good. Tragedy had no place in the picture. That memory lingers in my mind as a symbol of innocent joy, a kind of happiness I have not known since.

In one of my earlier books, I observed that something is wrong with everything. That observation, one that only those committed to pretending can deny, earned me in some circles the unflattering title of "Prophet of Doom and Gloom." But the title does not fit.

The *beginning* of the gospel is bad news, bad news about me and you and all of life. Something *is* wrong with everything. In response to a London newspaper's request that certain well-known figures answer the question, "What's wrong with the world?," G. K. Chesterton wrote: "Dear Sirs, I am! Sincerely, G. K. Chesterton." The *center* of the gospel, however, is good news: Christ died to forgive me and straighten me out. And the *end* of the gospel is sheer delight, for God and me.

But the end isn't ours to enjoy fully until the next life. Until then, the innocent joy of a happy childhood must yield to an embraced sadness in which mature joy can grow.

My father is a strange mixture of sadness and joy. He hurts, he gets discouraged, he struggles with the question that often bothers older folks: "What have I done of value with my life? Have I failed?" He is aware of his limitations. He knows that the beginning of the gospel is bad news that endures until the grave.

But he also rejoices in the center of the gospel. Every week he celebrates the Lord's Supper in order to keep the cross of Christ in the center of his attention. And he often says, "It's a mistake for older folks to spend too much time wistfully looking back on the good old days. For me, the best is still ahead." He understands the eternal end of the story, the end that his mother has been thoroughly enjoying for some time now.

I find it easy to pervert the beginning, center, and end of the gospel. I sometimes interpret the beginning as God's promise to me of a fulfilling life that will last forever. I misread the center as Christ's promise that his death on the cross guarantees my present fulfillment. And I see the end of the gospel as eternal fulfillment for me, with God as a beaming spectator. For years, I tried to convince myself that *my* life might never be touched by serious tragedy, that *my* soul could find satisfaction and rest in what Christians like to call the blessings of life. I had some reason to believe that lie.

I met a pretty girl when I was ten, had my first "date" with her when I was twelve, fell in love with her in my teens, and married her when I was twenty-one. Here we were, childhood sweethearts from godly families that had the same church background. We had two healthy, handsome, talented sons. I had earned a Ph.D. by the time I was twenty-five and had early opportunities that signaled a promising career. What more could anyone ask?

I can recall saying to my wife: "We've got so much going for us that if we play our cards right, things should really work out well for us." But that naïve hope soon crumbled. We live outside Eden, and evidence of that fact is all around us. Sometimes it slaps us in the face.

Within six months of our wedding day, Rachael's older brother Phil, and his wife, Lois, were killed in a plane crash, leaving four young children without parents. I remember watching John—Phil's best friend and the husband of one of Rachael's older sisters, a tall, good-looking Annapolis graduate who loved to laugh— reduced to tears by the force of tragedy. Watching him cry at the funeral is my most vivid recollection of that dark time.

I said earlier that the hardest thing I've faced so far in my life is the naked realization that I have no guarantees in this life except that God will be with me. God is not committed to keeping me healthy, financially secure, or satisfied with how family members treat me. But still I feel within me the familiar demand for a formula I can follow to get what I want. What can I do to obligate God to protect me from what I most deeply fear and to give me what I most passionately desire?

But there are no formulas. My grandmother did nothing that caused her husband's premature death. We can't study her life and say, "Ah, there's her mistake. If I make sure I don't make that same mistake, then my spouse will live a long time." We can't examine how godly adults were raised in order to reproduce a parenting pattern guaranteed to produce godly children. We can't respond to the heartbroken father who announces that his teenage son is in jail and ask ourselves, "What did those parents do wrong? If we're careful, we won't make the same mistake with our kids, and they can avoid getting arrested."

Unlike a seven-year-old at Christmas so many years ago, I now believe that tragedy is an undercurrent in everyone's life, with occasional eruptions that come with neither warning nor explanation. Life is more tragic than orderly. I must learn to quiet my soul, to hush, to learn the lesson of my grandfather's words, particularly when bad things happen or when I fear they might. When sleepless nights are plagued by sometimes irrational but always compelling fears, I must quiet myself and listen beneath the noise of my dread to the voice of someone whose goodness has not and will not waver. God is in it. His plan is good. I must believe it. And that must be the basis of joy, a mature joy that has lost the innocence of Eden but gained the security of hope.

Another thought occurs to me as I reread Dad's comments about his mother. I knew her. She died after I married. When I was thirteen, Grandmother lost most of her sight. With the insensitivity of a curious adolescent, I once asked her, "Grandma, what's it like to be blind?"

I'll never forget her answer. She looked at me with severe but compassionate intensity and simply said, "Larry, now that I can't see, I can pray so much better for you. There's less to interfere with my concentration." Quality of life mattered to her, but usefulness mattered more. And that gave her life an enduring quality that continues to affect me today.

As Dad writes of his mother, my thoughts naturally go toward mine. I've often been asked why I frequently tell stories of my father but rarely speak about my mother. Mother is a behind-the-scenes woman. She feels her central calling in life is to help her husband, and she honors that calling well.

Like so many women whose childhoods offered stable but not sentimental involvement, her tenderness and passion are more easily expressed through deeds than words. Unlike many people in my generation, Mother is more concerned with *loving* than with *saying,* "I love you." Her constant care for me spoke volumes that easy words never could. She made me hot tea when I was sick. She drove me to dermatologist appointments to get rid of acne and to speech therapy sessions because I stuttered. She "pegged" all my slacks on her sewing machine when pegged pants were the style.

My mother never demeaned me. When people ask her what it was like to raise me, she reliably says two things: "When he was little, he was a rascal," and "As he got older, I figured he was sensible and would make good decisions, so I didn't worry much about him." She disciplined me and believed in me.

Mother has a deep, tender dimension. A few days after my brother, Bill, died in 1991, Mother and I were standing in the kitchen of my home, preparing a snack. I forget the context for her remark, but I will never forget her words. She turned to me, and with a richly meaningful look that perhaps only hurt can produce, said, "I think all three of the Crabb men are pretty special."

I speak of her so rarely, I think, because she is not a public person. Her influence is like the Spirit's—rarely dramatic but always present. My appreciation for my mother is called forth as I hear my father express appreciation for his.

Two more thoughts come to mind as I reread my father's thoughts. First, Dad has an unusually rich inner life. And that means nearly constant struggle. He was aware of impressing the girls with his ball-playing ability. Every boy does it, but not many reflect on it. He admits to jealousy when his brother was sent away to an elite boarding school, but he turns that painful reality into an avenue of blessing: he became closer to his sister Helen, who shared his lack of advantage.

My second thought is this: Dad helps me define masculinity realistically. He was scared when he confronted the bully Johnny Rennick, and he didn't confront him until he first yielded to Johnny's insulting order to pull him in the wagon. The road to manhood includes both failure and fear. I'm still scared of certain things today, and no one but God knows how often I fail. But I'm still on the road to masculine maturity, largely because of Dad's example. I respect him as a *man:* he can be insecure, and he fails sometimes, but he is not weak. He continues to move into his world in whatever way he believes God directs him, passing on life from a soul that is far more alive than he thinks.

I recently asked him if he thought of himself as mature. He responded with embarrassment, as mature people often do. One hallmark of maturity is being more occupied with the One we're destined to resemble than with measuring our progress. God gives us something more fascinating to think about than ourselves. 🍂

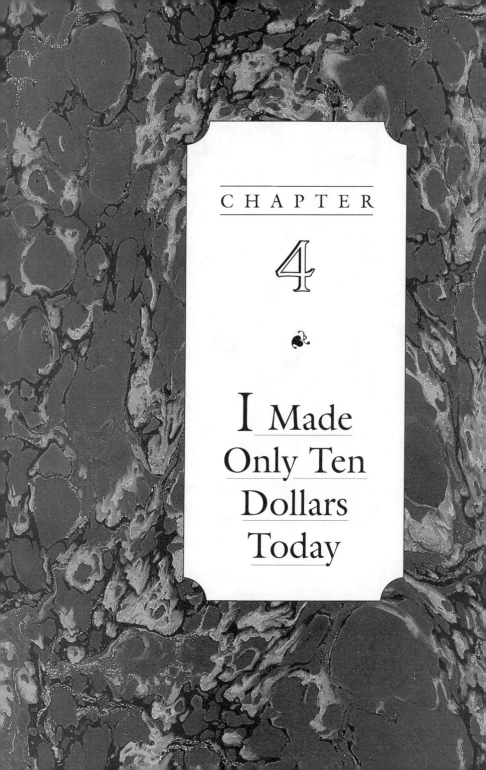

CHAPTER

4

&

I Made
Only Ten
Dollars
Today

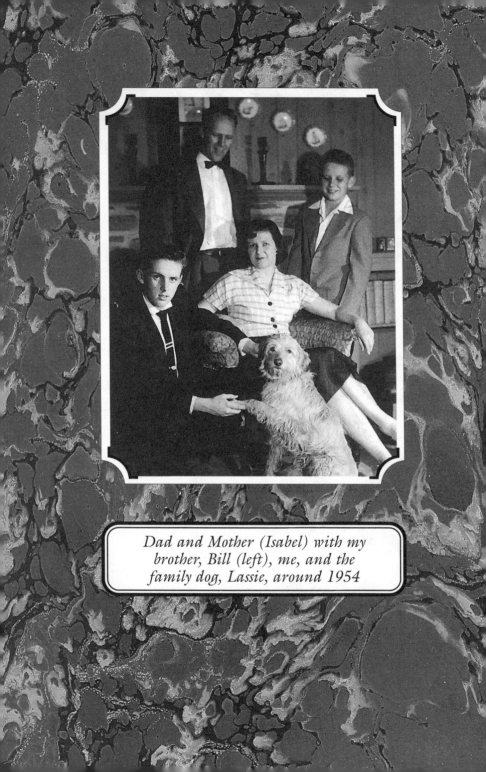

Dad and Mother (Isabel) with my brother, Bill (left), me, and the family dog, Lassie, around 1954

*If in this life only we have hope
in Christ, we are of all men most
miserable.*
1 CORINTHIANS 15:19 KJV

A Father's Recollections . . .

I n 1946, I left a good position with a major tool manufacturer in Chicago and began an industrial supply business in Philadelphia. Why had I given up a promising future with a really good company for this uncertainty?

I still wonder. I had started work in the company's Philadelphia branch and after about five years had been promoted to an executive position in the main office in Chicago. Things were going well. We had made friends in Chicago, and the suburban area where we had our home seemed ideal for our little family. By then we had two boys, Bill starting kindergarten, and Larry, Jr., just learning to walk.

Looking back, I can see it only as an itch to do things my way. Of course I prayed about it. I prayed over every major decision. Frankly, though, it's a bit amusing, pathetically amusing, as I think how God must have heard my pleas for guidance. The actual words were models of spirituality, but as I look back I can imagine God hearing a prayer something like this. "Dear Father, I have decided on my next move, and I'm sure you in your wisdom have seen my underlying motivation is to honor and please you. Now, if you'll just add your blessing. And may I remind you of your written promise to withhold no good thing from those who walk uprightly." I even reminded him that he could find those words in Psalm 84:11.

God did bless, but in a far more limited way than I so confidently expected. We always met the weekly payroll, but my take-home pay was nothing to brag about. Many days I put in long shifts, and when I left at night, I wondered if it was worth it. I remember the night I got into our car after work and announced to my wife with a discouraged sigh, "I made only ten dollars today."

My error, I see now, was in assuming that the relationships I had formed in Philadelphia, relationships formed when I was speaking for the company, would surely continue. Now I was just another dealer competing for customers. "How much can you save me? How soon can you deliver? Oh, we never pay cash!" And some who controlled purchasing by large accounts expected to be "taken care of."

Accounts receivable piled up; accounts payable piled up. Some days were good, but more days were bad. On too many days, our expenses exceeded our income.

Where was the God who had promised to "withhold no good thing"? I knew what "good" meant. Why didn't he cooperate? I had set up shop with such high hopes. I didn't see it at the time, but God must have seen something of Jacob's bargaining nature in me.

"You prosper me, and I'll reciprocate by furthering your kingdom." Can't you see God's amused smile as I continually reminded him of my plans to further *his* work, contingent, of course, on his cooperation in furthering *my* work?

I did work for him. Busy as I was in the business, I took a major part in spiritual activities. I acted as Sunday school superintendent and regularly took a group of boys on outings and witnessed to them fervently. Our home became a center for young people. I was the front man who organized activities and led in Bible studies, but Isabel did all the real work—the formidable task of feeding a group of several dozen young people every week—and she did it cheerfully. We were a team, a godly team doing his work in spite of crushing fatigue and discouraging finances.

Why wasn't God making good on his promise to open heaven's window and pour out his blessing, as he said in Malachi 3:10? We were keeping our end of the bargain.

I have known men who ran their own businesses, godly men, and I have seen their enterprises prosper. I have also known men who have gone through my shaky experience of bare survival. Why?

God just doesn't conform, just doesn't fit when we set him in a mold of our making. Characteristically, I suppressed the thought that perhaps I just didn't have what it takes, that running a business wasn't for me. A disturbing idea came from a reading of 1 Timothy 6:10. Could a "love of money" be the trouble? Was I wrong to wish so fervently to be free of the last-nickel pattern I had known so long? I wanted so little: "Give me neither poverty nor riches" (Prov. 30:8). Could I be wrong in wanting that? Surely God would grant so wise and reasonable a request.

I wondered whether God's idea of a healthy balance between poverty and riches would ever harmonize with mine. Neither the depths of poverty nor the heights of riches: how far removed from either extreme is the balance? The proverb might at least have specified how many shekels would comprise a reasonable income. Mystery is such an irritant. It requires trust when I'd rather plan.

How could I continue to provide for my family? How about the education of my two boys? I so longed for them to experience a better world than I had known: a world of Dickens, C. S. Lewis, Keats, Shelley, Bunyan. Must they too enter the work force in their early teens merely to survive?

All my anxiety was unnecessary. I can see it all so clearly now, years later. But then, even if the ninety-year-old apostle John had counseled me, I would have thought his advice was not at all pragmatic. Perfect love may cast out fear, but a healthy bank account does a good job too.

> *Somewhere over the rainbow*
> *Skies are blue,*
> *And the dreams that you dare to dream*
> *Really do come true.*

In that enduring fantasy *The Wizard of Oz,* Dorothy dared to dream of a wonderful land but found only the wizard, a pathetic dispenser of smoke and rumble. Is there a Santa Claus, a real wizard who will give us everything? Do the dreams that we dare to dream ever come true?

No, Virginia, there is no Santa Claus, but there is Someone far better. And yes, Dorothy, there is a wonderful land, a land that exceeds our fondest dreams: "Eye hath not seen, nor ear heard, neither have entered into the heart of man, the things that God hath prepared for them that love him" (1 Cor. 2:9 KJV).

I alternated between times of despair and times of firm confidence that God is good even when evidences of his goodness seemed painfully lacking. Unwavering confidence does not come easily.

"There is nothing to fear but fear itself." These words from the inaugural speech of Franklin Roosevelt are no platitude. *Fear of failure* is far worse than failure. Fear drains energy and too often justifies self-pity. I know. Oh, I did what every believer should do. I underlined biblical references to those truths that had seemed so helpful when I hadn't needed them. I read all the "fear nots" that our Lord often said to his timorous followers.

Only now do I dimly understand the force of Deuteronomy 33:27: "Underneath are the everlasting arms," the day-to-day provision by the same God who constantly replenished the widow's supply of food. Her barrel of flour was never used up, and her cruse of oil never went dry (1 Kings 17:15–16). Her needs were met in answer to faith and obedience, mine as a divine act of sheer grace.

But I kept asking the Lord for a larger reserve, larger helpings. I wanted security, solvency, something I could see. God offered no reply. But despite the agonizing silence of heaven, he always provided for the immediate circumstances.

When I was reading Job recently, a verse startled me: "The thing which I greatly feared is come upon me, and that which I was afraid of is come unto me" (Job 3:25 KJV). Note how verse 26 continues the litany: no rest, no quiet, only trouble. Do I misunderstand? Is Job saying, "God, I never presumed on your goodness, never presumed to enjoy your blessings. I knew all the time that every gift had strings attached"?

In my case God was providing. Somehow we paid the bills. Somehow, and this is so wonderful, both Bill and Larry, Jr., were able to complete college. I'm so proud of them; both earned doctorates solely through their own efforts.

Jacob differed from Job in that he had a problem with the way God handled situations. Can't you hear Jacob? "Just a minute, God, I have a better plan. I'd appreciate your cooperation as I do it my way." Isaiah talks about people who do it their way when he speaks of those who light their own fires to see in the dark. God's warning is pointed: "This shall ye have of mine hand; ye shall lie down in sorrow" (Isa. 50:11 KJV). How ridiculous it is to lie down in sorrow when he invites us to lie down in green pastures (Ps. 23). And yet I have done so time and time again. Why is trust, the kind that leads to quietness and rest, so hard to come by?

Mark 4 tells the story of Jesus asleep in the boat with his disciples. The weather was calm when they started out, but soon winds of hurricane force tossed the little boat about like a match stick. Immediately the disciples screamed for help, "Master, don't you care if we perish? How can you just lie there, asleep? Do something!"

I've been through this so many times. I've tried to be the captain of my own ship. Of course, I want the Lord to be aboard with me. He is entirely welcome, as long as he stays out of the way as I direct. If he chooses to help, fine. If not, he is free to take a nap. As long as the sea remains calm, I feel as if I don't need his help.

But suddenly, I'm in trouble: "I made only ten dollars today." Where is he? Now, years after the storm, with a wisdom of faith strengthened by experience, I assert what the Scripture has always said. He is there, always. He is good, always. And good *enough*. My part is to turn over the captain's post to him and to follow wherever he leads, even when it is not where I want to go.

A Son's Reflections . . .

I also remember the night Dad announced to Mother, "I made only ten dollars today." At the time he owned and managed Power Tool Company, a small business on Queen Lane in the Germantown section of Philadelphia. It wasn't a classy business address. No attorneys or CEO's had their offices nearby. Next to Power Tool on one side was an auto body shop, on the other side a coffee-and-donut-type diner.

But it was a clean street, filled with hard-working people making an honest living. The men my father employed were decent, friendly blue-collar workers, the kind who spent more time in the sports page of the *Philadelphia Evening Bulletin* than in the local library. My father's unceasing love for Keats and Dickens struck no resonating chord in any of them.

The four or five men with whom Dad spent every working day for years were a noisy, good-natured group who took special delight in ribbing the boss's younger son. I'm struck that, in spite of their natural coarseness, I never recall hearing an off-color joke or local bar language beyond an occasional "damn." I suspect that their respectable vocabulary and clean humor had less to do with their convictions and more to do with my father's convictions. Dad often spoke about the good influence Christians should have among their friends.

During college, I spent my summer and occasional after-school hours throughout the school year driving the delivery van for Power Tool. My brother's mechanical talents won him a job in the shop, repairing broken drills and routers and grinders. My gifts qualified me to sweep the floors and drive the van.

One of Dad's long-term employees was Roy, a lighthearted, personable black man who worked hard to feed his brood of four children. One summer day, after my first year of college had filled me with an insufferable sense of self-importance, I was standing with Dad as Roy bounced out of the shop at closing time with a cheery, "See you tomorrow."

I remember watching Roy climb into his old car, and with all the snobbish pity of royalty looking out the palace window at a street-vending commoner, I remarked, "I'll certainly not be wearing a blue collar around my neck when I'm thirty-five."

My father was a quiet man, reserved, not especially forward. But with a power that I've seen come out of him only a handful of times, he turned to me, glared, and, without raising his voice, said, "Whatever you have has been given to you. Never claim credit for it. Just use it well." Then he turned away.

On the day that Dad lamented his meager earnings, I was sitting in the back seat of our car. Mother was stationed behind the driver's wheel. He climbed in the passenger's side, and without even looking at my mother, said, "I made only ten dollars today." He looked so defeated, so entirely worn out. There was no spark, no friendly jousting with his son in the back seat, no touching Mother on her shoulder or hand, no smile. For the thirty-minute ride home and on into the evening, my father was absorbed by his discouragement.

I was only twelve at the time, and I had no understanding at all of the deep fear of failure that haunted him. I had no thought of doing whatever I could to lift him out of his despondency.

I do recall, though, that I was bothered by it. I wanted him to be happy and confident. It scared me to see him down. For reasons that are clearer now, I needed him to be up. Although I didn't consciously feel it at the time, I resented his discouragement. I didn't like the way it made me feel. If he couldn't handle life, what hope was there for me? After all, he was my father, the symbol of everything strong.

Perhaps if my father had died when I was five, I would remember him as he remembers his papa—ten feet tall, omniscient, omnipotent. But I've known my dad for forty-nine years. He stands five feet, eight inches tall; bigger dads could beat him up; he doesn't know everything; and bad times occasionally get to him.

Yet still I respect him immensely, more, I think, than he respects his father only because I have had more years to observe him. But why? Why do I so deeply respect this clearly imperfect man who worried about failing?

I'm certain I have illusions about my parents. What child of any age sees his or her parents objectively? We look at them as either better or worse than they really are, depending on a tangled collection of motives and memories. If our parents' primary effect on our souls has been good, we probably idealize them, more out of dependency and a need for them to continue feeding us than admiration. If their effect has been bad, we either inordinately idealize them to preserve a cherished illusion or harshly vilify them, seeing even their virtues as irremediably stained.

Whatever the cause, I respect my parents. I'm not blind to their shortcomings, and I recognize a few of the ways their impact on me could have been better, but still I respect them and love them deeply. Why?

One reason stands out above many others. Neither of them has yielded to discouragement. They have not left the path of responsible Christian living to find relief from their problems. I watched my father take his struggles to the Lord. He often remarked on King Hezekiah, who "held fast to the LORD and did not cease to follow him" (2 Kings 18:6). When troubles came in the form of a threatening letter from an enemy, Hezekiah "went up to the temple . . . and spread it out before the LORD" (2 Kings 19:14). My father didn't go up to the temple, but he often sat in his chair in front of the fireplace and spread it out before the Lord by reading his Bible and praying. The image sticks.

After worrying over a one-day profit of only ten dollars, the next Sunday morning Dad was at the Lord's Supper, not pretending that everything was as he wanted it, but grateful that the bottom line was good. He longed to know better the only source of real hope.

I've learned something from all this. The most profoundly good effect of a parent on a child does not come from consistent cheerfulness or self-confident strength or even from loving involvement that builds self-esteem. And it certainly does not depend on generous material provision. The most profoundly good effect of a parent on a child comes rather from the parent's unrelenting pursuit of God, a pursuit that continues through every setback of life.

That encourages me. My two sons have heard me say worse things than, "I made only ten dollars today." They have seen me discouraged to the point of immobility. They have felt an anger in me that eliminated compassion. They have observed me so worried that fear cast out all of love's comforting warmth. They have suffered under my self-serving demands that made their rebellion seem necessary.

I have done much that is good as a father. But I have also seriously failed. My failures have sometimes tempted me to quit. Why bother? Why try? I resolve to love well and be strong, and I do all that I know to do as a Christian, but still I hurt my wife. Still I give my sons a poor example of Christlike manhood, at best a corrupted taste of his powerful love.

But quitting is the only failure for which there is no recovery. Like my father (and largely because of him), I am pressing on, limping a bit, but still moving.

Perhaps in the midst of all the tangles in my relationship with my wife, with my sons, and with others who may be watching me, these folks will be encouraged to believe that trust in God is always legitimate and will one day be fully vindicated, even if today we make only ten dollars. 🙠

CHAPTER

5

I Don't
Want to Go
to Church
This Morning

*Mother and Dad at their fiftieth
wedding anniversary, 1988*

Behold how good and how pleas-
ant it is for brethren to dwell
together in unity!
PSALM 133:1 KJV

A Father's Recollections . . .

I have been associated all my life with those known as Plymouth Brethren. Each Sunday morning, the Lord's day, we meet to remember the Lord in what we speak of as the "Communion Service" or "Breaking of Bread." I have been a faithful attender for the past seventy plus years. More than habit, my attendance is a matter of conviction, based firmly on Scriptures such as Hebrews 10:25: Do not forsake "the assembling of ourselves together" (KJV).

But one Sunday morning about eight years ago, I didn't want to go to church, and I didn't.

Oh, I had my reasons—good ones, or so they seemed at the time. Frankly I hesitate to detail the reasons because honest reflection so often dims the validity of the positions I felt were so justified. The differences were on matters of procedure, specifics on which I stood firmly, quoting the apostle Paul as my authority as he spoke to young Timothy about proper behavior in

God's house (1 Tim. 3:11). After all, I was one of the older brethren, then in my seventies. Why didn't they acknowledge my wisdom, my spirituality, as I so graciously attempted to set them straight about the truth?

Those matters of procedure are not so clear today. What is still with me is *my* procedure that morning.

I was fidgety, restless. One moment I was determined to go to church; the next moment I was resistant. I was like the person James described: "A doubleminded man is unstable in all his ways" (James 1:8 KJV). Finally I determined that the grass needed cutting and worked almost feverishly on this for about half an hour. Then I found it necessary to clear up a mess I had left in the garage. Then the car needed to be washed. I did anything to avoid thinking about my deliberate decision to stay home when I knew I should be remembering my Lord as he had so clearly stated in his last request. This was no light matter.

Isabel wisely said very little. I knew she wouldn't go without me, yet I wished she would. If she had started out to church, I probably would have gone with her. Later she told me she had wanted to go, but she had dreaded the question, "Where's Larry today?"

How would she answer? "Oh, he's a bit put out with some of the things going on." Or, "He doesn't feel well." And she knew I needed her, perhaps as a sounding board, a vent for my frustrations.

Then, finally like the Prodigal Son in Luke 15, I came to myself. In fact, I started talking to myself, or, rather, I talked back to myself. Had I become a divisive element in the church? I thought about Christ's prayer for unity: "That they all may be one, even as we are one" (John 17:22 KJV). Was I like the Corinthian church members, who defended their separations with, "I am of Paul; and I of Apollos; and I of Peter; and I of Christ" (1 Cor. 1:12 KJV)?

Was I, were we, getting to the point at which only persecution could draw believers together? Can it be that we have sunk so low that many of our disputes are no more than camouflaged personality clashes? Have we become Pharisees, who "strain at a gnat, and swallow a camel" (Matt. 23:24 KJV)? Am I a Pharisee?

As I've grown older, I feel an increased yearning for a rich enjoyment of the gathering together in the oneness of the body of Christ. The participation of the members led by the Holy Spirit is so satisfying. One hymn writer, whom we know only by the initials C.A.W., expressed it well.

> *Gathered in Thy Name, Lord Jesus*
> *Losing sight of all but Thee,*
> *Oh, what joy Thy Presence gives us,*
> *Calling up our hearts to Thee.*

Does the Holy Spirit prompt this yearning in me? I want so much more than I often experience. Merely assembling is not the same as assembling *together*. Why does assembling together seem to be happening less frequently?

So often I head for a meeting with fellow believers, looking forward to enjoying together the presence of Christ. All it takes is one cool greeting or an imagined slight or an irritating comment, and the prospect evaporates as I react naturally, normally, sinfully. Fellowship becomes a distant relationship felt ever so faintly through layer on layer of platitudes. It's ironic to find the platitudes are often quotations from Scripture.

Yet I know real "layerless" fellowship is possible. I have experienced it over the years with many people. As I grow older and assimilate more of the Word, I wish I could initiate and foster what I read of as the "more excellent way" (1 Cor. 12:31). I want to remain above the petty problems that arise, yet I lack the wisdom to do it. And Scripture doesn't always give us clear-cut instructions about some things. Instead, it outlines the broad principles and leaves us to act in conformity with them.

Knowing God must be the path to a common enjoyment with fellow believers of all that God longs to give. When Moses wanted to meet God, God promised to commune with him at the mercy seat, between the two cherubim that crowned the ark of the testimony (Exod. 25:21). The typology is so fragrant with assurance of acceptance: the broken law, in the ark, but under the blood-sprinkled mercy seat. No one could uncover and look into the ark. No one could ever again bring up the law in condemnation of those covered by the blood of atonement.

The mercy-seat meeting with God is the basis of communion. To know more of this is to know God. Can individuals know God? Yes, delightfully so. But how wonderful to share this communion with other believers in a foretaste of the harmony of heaven. We must cherish and cultivate that which is so precious to our relational God. "Not forsaking the assembling of ourselves together, . . . and so much the more, as ye see the day approaching."

Things are becoming a bit foggy right now. It's about two in the morning. I seem to be dreaming, dreaming I am on a high elevation, supported rather unsubstantially by a cloud. It's really rather pleasant here as I sit enjoying my mastery of "essential" doctrines of the faith: dispensationalism as opposed to covenant theology; premillennialism, clearly the only tenable view of eschatology.

Suddenly I feel a sensation of free fall. As I descend, I see doctrinal convictions floating all around me. I seem strangely unconcerned as I watch so much that I had thought of as rock-solid doctrines now moving about with no visible anchor. The fall has just ended with a soft landing on a firm foundation so much different from the earlier cloud base.

How clear the air is down here, no fog, no mist. Far above me I see the convictions I still adhere to, but now I don't feel so attached to them, so bound to them, so stubborn about them. Here in the clarity of purer air, I see the possible validity of viewpoints other than my own. It's all somewhat humbling, but it seems to be creating in me a new openness, a new understanding of people who fail to dot their *i*'s and cross their *t*'s as I think they should.

I am now looking down. What is this new, warmly solid ground? My foundation is made up of those truths without which there is no relationship with God, no standing before him: truths of the Lord Jesus Christ, his deity, his eternal sonship, salvation solely of grace through the finished work of Calvary.

"It is finished" was a shout of triumph signaling the end of all that held God back from his yearned-for enjoyment of his creatures. Without this shout and all that is behind it, Christianity is meaningless. It offers nothing. But with Christ's shout of triumph, Christianity offers everything. This is essential truth. All those doctrinal positions I previously held as essential have not lost importance but are now seen in perspective. I realize that they are not worth causing dissension and bitterness between those who truly know and love the Savior.

Perhaps I had seen doctrine as a support structure of solid poles holding us up, rather than pipes through which God pours out his love toward us. In falling to a lower level of self, perhaps I have been brought to an appreciation of the deeper meaning of doctrine: a body of teaching that tells the story of a love affair, a one-sided romance about Someone who never wavers in his pursuit.

> *How little worthy of any love thou art!*
> *Whom wilt thou find to love ignoble thee,*
> *Save Me, save only Me?*
> *All which I took from thee I did but take,*
> *Not for thy harms,*
> *But just that thou might'st seek it in My arms.*
> *All which thy child's mistake*
> *Fancies as lost, I have stored for thee at home:*
> *Rise, clasp My hand and come!*
>
> *(From "The Hound of Heaven" by Francis Thompson)*

Without relationship, which is the very center of Christianity, all our doctrines are no more than sounding brass or tinkling cymbals. I still don't want to "go to church." But I do long for relationship with Christ and to enjoy that relationship with others who know him too.

A Son's Reflections . . .

A famous preacher once said that burying his father gave him a sense of freedom he had never known before. Every son, I suspect, feels at least a little trapped by an inescapable longing for his father's approval, a longing that for many men survives their fathers' death.

Dad and I don't agree on everything. Our spending habits are different. I think nothing of buying the pair of socks I like. Only a ridiculous price tag would stop me. Dad would be more inclined to buy a pair he didn't like quite as well if they were less expensive.

If someone were to list fifty points of theology, we would take different positions on a few. We might disagree on which points deserve more emphasis and which points are indisputable. For example, Dad is firmly committed to certain principles of local church functioning, and I hold these principles with much more flexibility.

In my late twenties, I joined an evangelical church that did things very differently from the Plymouth Brethren group in which I was raised. It took me six months to decide to join that church, and I cried several times during those agonizing months over the prospect of abandoning my heritage.

Looking back, I wonder if at least some of the emotion came from a nagging sense of disloyalty to my father. His convictions about church life matter to me. They did then, they do now, and they will, I expect, after he dies.

Why? Why do they matter as much as they do? Do I feel trapped by them, pressured to conform in order to win his approval? Or is it more a matter of respect for his wisdom, a respect similar to a young doctor's respect for the opinion of a seasoned surgeon?

The latter is certainly a large part of it. I greatly respect my father. I feel the freedom to disagree with his views; but I would never do so lightly. It wouldn't make sense. He has wisdom that can be gained only through long years of honest living and continual preoccupation with God's Word.

But the desire for his approval still lingers within me, perhaps more than I can or care to admit. The longing for an approving smile from the man who from my earliest years represented life-giving power is strong. It will not go away. The result is a dynamic in every father-son relationship, a dynamic that breeds tension, a dynamic that gets in the way of productive mentoring.

Let me theorize for a minute. The dynamic consists of two elements. First is the father's sense that his son has betrayed him when the son makes decisions the father would not make. Good fathers, like mine, want their children to think for themselves and choose their own directions. But fathers tend to value *right* decisions over *free* decisions. What father would not prefer that his son choose hard work over freely electing the life of a drifter? Fathers want their sons to choose freely, but they hope that clear thinking will prevail and that their sons will independently conform to their ideas.

Can you name an ardent Democratic father who is fully pleased with his son's Republican leanings because they represent careful thought? Can you imagine a father with deep Baptist roots feeling as proud at his son's ordination into the Presbyterian ministry as he would if his son were being ordained into a Baptist church? The rub, of course, is that fathers believe their sons' welfare is best served by conformity to the fathers' convictions. "He *must* make the right decision! I want it for *him!*" I wonder how many of us violate the first commandment but call it loving our sons: "You must serve God as I interpret him for you"?

The second element in this dynamic is a son's felt need to establish distance between himself and the man with whom he most wants to be close. The see-saw tips one way or the other. Either the son makes choices because they go against his father's wishes, or he sacrifices autonomy and does whatever his father wants because his father wants it. In neither case is he free. He remains carefully perched on one end of the see-saw, reacting to his father on the other end.

Now this really is a mess. The father wants a legacy; the son wants autonomy. The father feels betrayed when his son exercises his freedom in a way that robs the father of his legacy. The son spends his life caught in the tension of wanting both independence and approval. To gain approval, he must cooperate with his father's view of life; but to feel independent, he must violate it.

No real mentoring can take place until this dynamic is resolved. Until then, the father's attempts to mentor will feel like pressure to the son, who will then either rebel or capitulate.

My father's struggle over his decision to stay home from church one Sunday morning may have pointed to perhaps the only path out of this tangle. In his "vision" (maturity always leads away from rationalism to mysticism) he saw all his fondly held theological positions floating about him as he fell through space. *These doctrines were no longer capable of supporting him on a high place.* Now that is an important point. And because they were no longer supporting him in the elevated position that was now gone, losing them presented no real threat to him. He still believed his viewpoints, but he did not need them to be true and therefore did not need others to hold to them. Dialogue became possible.

When his fall ended and he finally landed, he found himself on a firm but comfortable surface that reminded me of green pastures by cool waters. His former perch was built of strenuously held academic viewpoints on important but not central matters. The new foundation (which was his all the time) consisted of a warm relationship with the Savior, a deeply personal relationship that he could extend to others and enjoy with them.

I like his imagery. The perch was supported by poles (doctrinal viewpoints) that, when he fell to a new foundation, became pipes through which love could flow. His convictions remained the same. But the purpose and usefulness of the convictions changed.

As long as his views on church life (or anything else) are solid poles that keep him elevated above others, his efforts to influence the world will be felt as pressure that will either incite rebellion or promote compliance. But when his doctrinal positions become more like open pipes carrying God's love, his statement of them will encourage dialogue and, what is more important, will invite others into deeper relationship. The effect will be more harmony and less division.

I still differ with Dad on a few things. Occasionally, the way he argues his positions makes them seem more like solid poles than open pipes. And sometimes I feel that I am fighting to maintain independence, foolishly thinking that separateness from him will make me more of a man. Other times I ignore my ideas and gauge my plan of action according to what I think he would like, thinking, with equal foolishness, that his approval is a source of life.

But we share common convictions: that we are each responsible to please our Lord and not each other; that deeper relationship with the Lord is the prize we're both after; that legitimate division occurs only when there are different understandings on how that relationship is first secured. And we don't differ on that.

With these convictions firmly in place and always deepening, we continue to bore out the poles and turn them into pipes through which God's love can freely flow in our relationship.

Whatever increase in freedom I may feel when he dies will be less, immeasurably less, than my sense of loss. ❧

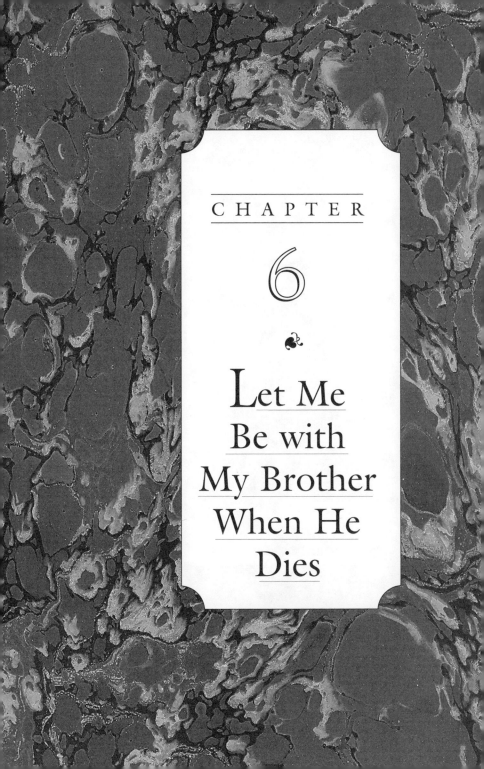

CHAPTER

6

Let Me
Be with
My Brother
When He
Dies

Dad and my uncle, Cecil, 1916

Lord, to whom shall we go?
thou hast the words of eternal
life.

A Father's Recollections . . .

After Mother died, the "we five" became "we four": my brother, Cecil; my two sisters, Helen and Mabel; and me. All of us married and had children. We were separated geographically but were still very much a family.

I still thought of Cecil as my big brother, the first baseman of our sandlot ball team. We still bragged about those days in the 1920s. I remember the day Cecil rescued me from a beating I was getting from a real fighter. I had just taken one on the nose when Cecil arrived on the scene, just like the Lone Ranger. I was so relieved to see him.

The years had brought us even closer. We forgot our childhood disagreements: "Why can't you leave my things alone?" "This is my room!" "It's just as much mine as yours."

Cecil had retired from his work as a chemist with the DuPont Company, and he and his wife, Gennie, were looking forward to travel and a comfortable life because of Cecil's substantial pension. They planned to travel through the U.S. as well as visit England and South America.

But then Cecil developed a health problem. It turned out to be a cancer that required amputation of Cecil's leg. Suddenly all of life changed.

I still remember how placidly, even cheerfully he accepted his new life. "Why should I complain?" he responded. "I've enjoyed the past seventy-plus years. I can still read. I can still tinker with my computer. And I still have Gennie."

He did live a full life. He taught literature to adults. He had one son, Charlie, with whom he was very close, and Frank, a lifelong friend who had been second baseman of our boyhood baseball team. Frank helped Cecil learn to use his artificial limb. Because Cecil's amputation was above the knee, he found it difficult to get around. Frank spent countless hours of countless days patiently encouraging Cecil during those difficult times.

A few years after Cecil's amputation, Isabel and I retired to South Carolina, but we often traveled to New Jersey to visit my brother. Always we found a house full of company. Cecil and Gennie liked people, and people liked them. I always looked forward to these visits, even though Cecil and I had gone different ways, not only geographically but also philosophically.

I had long ago accepted Jesus Christ as Savior. Cecil chose differently. He thought of himself as an agnostic, certain of the impossibility of knowing anything beyond the obvious facts of this life.

We went over this time and time again. I found it discouraging that my brother, with whom I shared so many memories, who had been the object of my mother's prayers, was still a stranger to God. I resent Christians who speak of the wickedness of people who do not believe as they do. I'm certainly biased, but everyone who knew Cecil liked and trusted him. He made no pretense of Christianity, but he evidenced so many virtues we often narrowly think of as the special province of professing Christians.

Then the cancer resurfaced. Endless medication led to no improvement. Cecil was again in the hospital. We formed a team to stay with him around the clock, and we felt occasional glimmers of hope. When the doctors arranged to remove a cataract from Cecil's left eye, we said to each other, "Surely the medical experts know more than they are telling; why would they schedule such an operation for a terminally ill patient?"

Only a day later the doctors released Cecil and sent him home, saying they could do nothing more for him. Now there was only medication, an ordeal in itself for one who had been through so much. We had lots of questions: Is this giving up? What purpose will the continued medication serve? Wouldn't it be better to do only what will make his last days more comfortable?

The only response the medical people gave us was, "We're sorry, but we can't predict what his future will be at this time."

I thought it was his last day. I still remember it vividly. Kneeling by his bedside, I quietly asked, "Cecil, would you like me to pray with you?" The medical staff had asked us not to mention death to Cecil. He had reacted badly when even the hint was given, but he knew. For so many years he had resented the slightest implication that death meant any more than an end to existence.

But as I mentioned prayer, he looked at me with tears filling his eyes. I had never seen him cry. "Larry, I'd like that. Yes, I'd like that."

You would think that I would remember every detail of this profound experience, yet surprisingly I can't recall the prayer I offered that day. Could it be that the words I used were not mine? Could it be that "The Holy Spirit pray[ed] for us with such feeling that it cannot be expressed in words" (Rom. 8:26 TLB)?

That same day the doctor in charge examined Cecil and told us, "We can't be certain, but we think Cecil will linger for some time. We can make him comfortable, and let you know when we think the end is imminent." Isabel and I decided to make the journey home to South Carolina. We had many things to do after our long stay in New Jersey, and Gennie promised to call us immediately if any change occurred.

We didn't say good-bye but rather, "Be seeing you soon," our usual expression at parting. The long ride home was filled with thoughts of Mother's faith as I fervently prayed and asked God, "Let me be with my brother when he dies!" I wanted to be there, to speak of Christ as my big brother passed into eternity.

We arrived home late that night, still pleading with God, repeating the same prayer. The night was long, and I found I couldn't sleep.

Early the next morning Gennie called. She could only say, "Cecil is gone." (How we try to avoid the terrifying word *death*. We speak of those who have "gone before," those who are "no longer with us," those who have "departed this scene.")

Cecil was dead. My big brother was dead.

Where was God? I had asked him to allow me to be with my brother when he died. He had said no to my plea.

I looked back a half-century and could see Mother smiling through her tears, speaking to the four of us beside the bed from which my papa would never rise. "Children, Papa will get well. You'll see. God answers prayer. He is able." I was just a child then, a boy of five. But who would question Mother's faith? Papa would get well. God was able. He had even raised the dead.

In the many years since that day at my father's bedside, I had supposed my faith had matured to the point where I could trust God no matter what. But now, all those old questions resurfaced, and I struggled to believe, to accept that God was good and caring.

I had not asked God to spare Cecil; perhaps that was too much even to hope, let alone pray for. He had terminal cancer. My prayer was so reasonable, a concession to the God I had so staunchly defended as omnipotent. I simply asked: "Let me be with my brother when he dies." And here I was hundreds of miles away. I could only shake my head and get ready for the return trip to New Jersey to attend his funeral.

My faith tottered, but it was not completely shattered. I survived only because I knew that I could go to the Lord for strength: "To whom else shall we go?" (John 6:68 KJV). That my faith survived at all is witness to God's mercy in not revealing the future. Had I known then that this deep hurt would soon be followed by my sister's death and then the sudden death of my son Bill, I might well have echoed poor Job as quoted by one of his comforters: "Behold, he findeth occasions against me, he counteth me for his enemy, he putteth my feet in the stocks" (Job 33:10–11 KJV).

We drove back to New Jersey for the funeral, the second funeral for one of the "we five" who survived my father's death. Of my father's funeral, I recall nothing except Mother's words: "Papa's with the Lord. We'll see him soon." At my mother's funeral we were comforted to remember that Mother believed the Rapture was always imminent; she regularly placed her Bible on the dining room table, open to 1 Thessalonians 4 as explanation of Papa's absence and as hope for reunion.

Cecil's funeral was handled as well as one could wish. People paid tribute to a gentle man, to a man meriting respect from all who knew him. The church gave all that it could to comfort. A large crowd at both the viewing and the burial ceremony convincingly spoke of so many who loved Cecil, who missed him.

Looking back, however, I remember the funeral as bleak, somber, so different from those I had attended, even participated in, where the prospect of reunion in heaven dominated. In those funerals, comfort came through thoughts of the Rapture, of being forever with the Lord, promises so exactly spelled out in God's Word, especially in 1 Thessalonians 4 and 1 Corinthians 15.

Still, I felt some hope. The Holy Spirit had prayed for Cecil. I would see him again. He and I would be together with Mother and Papa. Wasn't this the lesson of the Prodigal Son who "came to himself"? As he began the long walk back, his father saw him in the distance and began running—imagine God running—to welcome his son *home!*

Someone has said, "We stand in the perilous place where faith is often discovered," in that place where the only viable alternative is to cling to God. "He that cometh to God must believe that *he is*, and that he is a rewarder of them that diligently seek him" (Heb. 11:6, emphasis added, KJV). Like a drowning man, I have often echoed that plea: "Lord I believe, help my unbelief." I know what it is to reach out in darkness to the only source of light.

At Cecil's funeral, and since, I have reached out to that light. But no bells rang, no lightning struck from above. Instead, an indefinable calm has eased through my soul, creating a mooring that has remained firm. My desperate plea, "Let me be with my brother when he dies," has been replaced by a quiet trust.

Centuries ago, a dying man cried out to another dying Man, "Lord, remember me." The answer from the One who came to seek and to save those who are lost stirs me with the wonder of his eager grace: "Today shalt thou be with me in paradise" (Luke 23:43 KJV).

My one surviving sister and I have frequently spoken together of these things. To those who speak often in his name, the Lord truly gives songs in the night. I was not with my brother when he died. But today, through an ache that continues, my heart can sing.

A Son's Reflections . . .

In my worst moments, when confusion slips into angry disillusionment, I sometimes cry out, "God, I know you're good. But what good are you?" Exactly what is he supposed to be doing when his child disappears into the mud, unable to find anything firm on which to stand?

My father recently underwent open heart surgery. The main valve that opens to release blood into the body had thickened. Not enough blood was getting out. And one major vessel carrying blood into the heart was clogged. The surgeons sawed through his chest bone to replace the bad valve and to perform a single bypass. All this on an eighty-year-old man, in excellent health, but still eighty.

I was with Dad before the surgery and again shortly after. Before the surgery he was cheerfully resolute but not lighthearted. He had no doubt that if he failed to survive the operation he would be with the Lord and the rest of his family. But his mood reflected a steady apprehension, an apprehension that perfect love did not cast out.

Afterward, when the operation was declared a success, he still struggled. The physical struggle was far worse than any of us anticipated. He could hardly walk. When he coughed to loosen phlegm, the movement would jar the newly hinged chest bone and produce searing pain. Then an endless stream of cheerful nurses poked and prodded into his already chewed-up veins to draw yet more blood.

He felt personal struggles too. What does spiritual victory look like in an eighty-year-old man recovering from open heart surgery? How does maturity handle emotional anguish that begs for help in words like these: "God, relieve the pain. And if you won't do that, at least give me some taste of your presence, some experience that unmistakably lets me know you're here."

A month after his surgery, he told me, "You really don't know all that's gone through my mind since the operation. One night, when I was in sheer agony, I told God how unfair it was that I was born two thousand years after Christ was on earth. Had I been alive when he was here in the flesh, he could have walked up to me, placed his hand on my chest, and fixed things without all that blasted cutting. I know that kind of thinking is irrational, but desperation rarely breeds clear thought. All I wanted was relief, and God was not cooperating."

He went on to say, "So many of the hymns we sing today are misleading. Some are just plain silly. When things are bad, our experience doesn't measure up particularly well to all the joy and confidence we so warmly sing about."

Is that victory? Is that maturity? Paul sang at midnight when he was in jail. But he later spoke of intense, unrelieved loneliness. And Jeremiah went through mood swings that today would be diagnosed as serious instability needing strong medication.

Should we make ourselves sing when our hearts are filled with sorrow? Must we berate ourselves for weak faith when we can't get out one melodic note? Perhaps the richest song is the expression of an unrelenting confidence in God's goodness even when we see absolutely no visible evidence to support it. Maybe the songs of deepest worship grow out of the darkest nights.

During my father's ten-day hospital stay, he did not sleep well. For several nights he shared a room with a patient whose snoring could wake the dead. One night the nurses gave Dad some sleep medication, but it had a disastrous effect on him. Rather than put him to sleep, it made his mind race uncontrollably in bizarre directions to the point where he hallucinated. For four hours, he was psychotic, unable to take charge of his thinking.

I hated to see him suffer. When he coughed, I wanted to leave the room. It was difficult to watch him grimace with unbearable pain and then to see him force a reassuring smile. Sometimes he simply had no energy left for a smile.

One night I returned to my hotel room very anxious about my dad. I neither read nor watched television. Instead, I prayed fervently for more than an hour. "God, let him sleep tonight." I knew God had the ability to put him to sleep. And I knew that if I had that same ability, I would do it.

I returned to the hospital the next morning, eager to find out how the night went. I'm not sure what I expected. I think I felt an angry confidence: Of course God had made him sleep. Why wouldn't he?

I greeted my mother as I entered his room. She had spent the night in that small room with him, unwilling to accept my offer of a private hotel room. She slept, as she had every night since the surgery, on a reclining chair that allowed no turning over to get comfortable. She looked tired, more tired than usual.

"How did he sleep?" I asked.

"Terribly," she replied, this time without a hopeful smile. Her voice had lost its usual determined optimism. She was exhausted.

I spent the day in the hospital room, watching Mother hover over Dad with energy she didn't have. I listened to him cough, then wince with pain. I helped him get out of bed for the required but dreaded walks around the nurses' station. I was there when six white-clad personnel stormed into his room and pushed me into the hallway, along with Mother and my sister-in-law Phoebe, when Dad's heart threatened to give up.

He survived the emergency. Afterward, one nurse commented, "He'd do so much better if he could just get a decent night's sleep." I wanted to scream.

That night, back in the hotel, I again began to pray, "God, let him sleep tonight. Please!" But this time I couldn't go on. I stopped after one sentence, over-whelmed with a smothering sense of futility. Why bother? I still believed that God cared. The Cross won't let me escape that conclusion. I had no doubt that the God who called the world into being with a word could cer-tainly put a tired man to sleep. But I believed all that the night before, when I had prayed for an hour. And noth-ing had happened then. Why should things be different now?

I was confronted with an enraging mystery. In spite of my prayers to a powerful, good God, I could see nothing supernatural in my father's recovery. No doctor was stunned by anything that normal medical categories couldn't explain. I think if someone had told me that my father would sleep if I had the faith to believe he would, I might have hit him. Glib answers that make God pre-dictable infuriate me.

But why couldn't God do just one miracle, and a small one at that. Sleeplessness should present no obsta-cle to one who brought a dead man out of his grave and made a lame man leap. I could see no reason for God to refuse my request. One good night's sleep. Surely that wasn't too much to ask.

As I lay on that hotel bed, alone, weary, burdened for my parents and disappointed with God, a strange sense came over me: I knew God wanted to speak. I could not pray with confidence for Dad to sleep well, but it suddenly occurred to me that perhaps I shouldn't. That confidence was not warranted. I wanted to be confident that I could persuade God to do something; I was not willing to be confident in *who God is, regardless of how he behaves.*

I picked up a G. K. Chesterton book, *Faith: The Romance of Orthodoxy,* a book I had read several times already but had brought along on this trip for no clear reason. I turned to a portion in which Chesterton described the kind of person he had discovered Christ to be. I eagerly read his comments, wanting to enjoy an uncooperative God.

I felt within my soul a shift: instead of demanding control over God, I found myself pleading for an encounter with Christ. That night something happened. I caught a glimpse of Christ. I sensed a compassion so real that not even thoughts of my father's suffering could weaken it. I was awed by a strength that was invincible, a power that could not be harnessed by a mere man. I felt caught up in the reality of someone I could trust. I rested, for just a moment, in the middle of unrelieved turmoil.

God did not answer my prayer. But he gave me a glimpse of his Son.

God did not arrange for Dad to be with his brother when he died. He could have, but he didn't. And he didn't give my father one good night's sleep in the hospital. Dad has been home now for more than a month, and he has yet to enjoy a really good sleep. I see no unarguable evidence for the supernatural in either the timing of my uncle's death or my father's recovery from surgery. But still I believe that God was at work in both events.

Through the ache of unanswered prayer over his brother's death, my father can sing, not silly songs that speak of an easy confidence that God will always come through as we wish he would, but the richer melody that haunts the souls of those who have caught a glimpse of Christ. And though my struggles and questions continue, I occasionally can hear the same tune. Even when I can't, I believe it's still playing somewhere. ❧

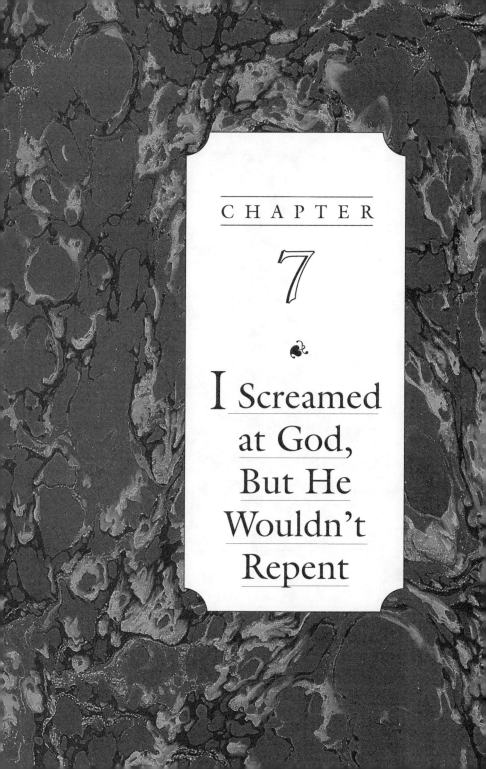

I Screamed at God, But He Wouldn't Repent

My brother, Bill, 1969

My feet had almost slipped;
I had nearly lost my foothold.
PSALM 73:2

A Father's Recollections . . .

It was Sunday morning, March 3, 1991. The telephone rang, and Isabel answered it. Then I heard her scream, "Larry, pick up the phone! Something terrible has happened. I'm not sure what. Hurry!"

It was Phoebe, our son Bill's wife. Her voice was frantic, almost incoherent. "I'm at the airport. Bill was so close; they tell us only that the plane has crashed."

Later that morning we heard the official word: *"No survivors."*

No survivors? How can that be? Our son, *our* son was on that plane!

Why? Why, God? *Why?*

I didn't know what to do with the feelings raging inside me. I went out to the field behind our house, and I screamed at God for ten minutes. I paced back and forth, questioning, even denying the goodness of the omnipotent God.

As I screamed at the open heaven, hoping to be heard by an ever-present God—my Father, the One I had trustfully addressed as Papa—I saw only a sky, a silent, empty sky. God, it seemed, was hiding. He was mute.

Bill was dead. Why, God? Why?

In the echo of my screaming at God, I heard my father's words: "Hush! God is in it."

Now I am faced with the same choking sorrow that Mother knew over seventy years ago. How real are those words that once hung on the wall of that tiny house in Philadelphia, words printed and framed in tears, indicating a rare faith.

Papa told us to hush in the presence of death. My immediate reaction was to scream.

Does the bitterness of my screaming sadly show how close I am to questioning God's sovereignty and goodness? Can this be, for me, the sin that so easily besets (Heb. 12:1)? I wish that I could share my papa's confident words as he was welcomed into glory, as he left behind a heartbroken wife of less than ten years and four little ones.

When life was pleasant I often spoke of the delightful unpredictability of God. But when tragedy strikes and faith wavers, how quickly I tend to see his sovereign plan as anything but delightful.

They say time heals all, but the platitude is unconvincing. About a year after that appalling morning of his death, the ache within me compelled me to write Bill a letter. Of course I never mailed it. I knew the address, but who could make the delivery?

Dear Bill:

Perhaps you can read this even as I write. How little we earth-bound people know of life as you now know it. Ours is a blend of life and death. You know only life—Life! How well you must know *him* by now.

I take comfort in two truths our Father gives. "Absent from the body . . . present with the Lord" and "To be with Christ . . . is far better" (2 Cor. 5:8 and Phil. 1:23 KJV). I have no question but that you are happy in a way I'll never know until I join you in heaven.

I sometimes wonder if you know how we miss you. Only yesterday you were so much a part of us. To ask why a loving Father should take you in the prime of a useful life is not to question but rather to ask for insight into the divine will. Will this ever be granted or must we blindly trust?

Blindly trust? No!

Can we trust blindly in light of what is so clear of God's character? Who can doubt the love of One who gives himself incarnate—even unto death? No! It is an affront even to speak of blind trust.

How I envy you. One terrible instant and then— and here I am supremely confident—a sudden emerging into reality, the fulfillment of all your most impossible dreams. Was it as C. S. Lewis supposes, just as you, without knowing, always knew it *must* be? Were you to return, even for a moment, would you like Paul find it impossible to describe the indescribable?

Always, always, Bill, as I think of you, I see you in the presence of Truth himself. I know you are with him. What more could I wish for you than is now yours? Yes, I miss you, as so many do, but my sorrow is overwhelmed in the certainty of the cheering promise, "The dead in Christ shall rise first:

111

then we which are alive and remain shall be caught up together with them in the clouds, to meet the Lord in the air: and so shall we ever be with the Lord" (1 Thess. 4:16–17 KJV). *Together!*

Be seeing you—soon.

Dad

Even as I wrote this letter, I felt a delightful sense of knowing God, a passionate realization of his nearness. Why must such moments be so strange, so hard to put into words? God, delightfully unpredictable, makes himself known in such moments, moments when we need him desperately, moments when no one else, nothing else will do.

No survivors! When the numbing shock of those words forced their way into our consciousness, God gave Isabel and me a glimpse of the reality beyond: a whiff of heaven. At the time of our son's death, we were a happily married couple with a history of fifty-two years of "togetherness." We were close. I couldn't imagine being closer. But God had promised that he would give to all who mourn "beauty for ashes" (Isa. 61:3). How can I express the new oneness we experienced as we held each other that Sunday morning? We felt an intense unity that will be exceeded only in heaven.

"They will become one flesh." We enjoyed, in those moments, a taste of the sheer other-centeredness that will one day stamp each of God's children. One day we will not only be with him but also be *like* him. The wonder of those moments of closeness amidst the ashes of our son's death was truly a whiff of heaven.

God is good. He is kind. No matter how I may question his acts, they are part of his ways, part of his master plan. Bill is undeniably alive and well, beyond the shadow, a shadow that God himself will soon burn away in the sunshine of the coming of his Son.

I wrote a few thoughts in my journal the morning after I wrote my letter to Bill: "How can I go on? It's fantastic, fabulous, beyond any words I can invent. My son Bill is there. He is *there*. This I know!"

I pictured Bill as he suddenly entered into the presence of the Lord: "Welcome home, Bill." For Bill, the fullness of the Lord's presence is real. For me, now, only a whiff.

Before Bill's death, I was so sure I had matured, that God's delightful unpredictability was a conviction, an unshakable reality. But I'm afraid my response would warrant the rebuke Eliphaz gave to his friend Job: "Behold thou hast instructed many, and thou hast strengthened the weak hands. . . . But now it is come upon thee, and thou faintest; it toucheth thee, and thou art troubled" (Job 4:3, 5 KJV).

May the experiences I have had since Bill's death renew my confidence in God's goodness. May my confidence in God's character grow so that I can think of Bill's death and say with Job, "The LORD gave, and the LORD hath taken away; blessed be the name of the LORD" (Job 1:21 KJV).

A Son's Reflections . . .

It seems strange, but I felt loved as I read my father's reaction to the news of Bill's death. And perhaps more strangely, I felt put in my place.

Dad's passion for Bill runs deep. One day months after the crash, Dad had to pull the car over to the side of the road. Thoughts of Bill provoked so much emotion, he couldn't drive. Had I died, he would have felt the same enormity of loss. That makes me feel loved.

But as I read Dad's letter to Bill, I noticed that his mind seemed to be occupied less with missing Bill and more with the thought of Bill seeing Christ. More than once in conversation with me, he has broken eye contact to stare into a world of his own and in a voice of hushed awe said, "To think that Bill has actually seen him. What that must be like!"

On one of those occasions, he went on to reflect, "We make a mistake when we try to imagine what Christ looked like as a man. Scripture never tells us. When we see him, we'll know him because of who he is, not because he'll look like some painting we've seen. His actual appearance will simply express the wonder of his character. Even the nail prints in his hands won't be required. The force of his person will mark him immediately."

Sometimes our family reminisces about Bill. But the conversation reliably drifts toward Christ, not because we can't handle the pain that memories bring, but because we're drawn to the One who has removed the sting of death. If I had died, conversation about me would move in the same direction, away from me, toward Christ. And that puts me in my place.

I drove to the cemetery on the day we buried Bill. Rachael was next to me in the front seat, and my parents were in the back. During the hour drive my father remarked, "You know, it wouldn't be wrong if today we laughed at something funny. The tragedy is real, but death will not win. We could tell a joke without being flippant or irreverent because our reason for celebration hasn't diminished. Lightheartedness can be a part of terrific grief. The loss is terrible, but the story ends well."

For Dad, relationships have always mattered deeply, but an unseen relationship mattered more. Maybe that's a good summary of parenting: make sure your kids know they're loved, but never put them in the place of God. That place can never be shared.

It was this kind of parenting that turned my brother's life around. If he were writing a chapter in this book, he would tell us his story. Let me see if I can tell it as he would tell it. I think I know him well enough to try.

I don't know why I resisted the Lord for as long as I did, but I do know what brought me back. One night, when I was in my early thirties, I was walking down the hallway of our home late at night. Phoebe was asleep in our bedroom, and Caryn and Curtis, ages five and three, were each asleep in theirs. I stopped at Caryn's door and then Curt's. I opened their doors and stared at each child for several minutes. These were my children, my daughter and son.

With a force that hit me with sudden impact, I realized that one day they would grow up. They would make choices about what to believe and how to live. Then I realized that I had nothing to tell them; I didn't know what I believed about life.

115

I felt cold, terrified, and utterly alone. I had no clear commitment to Christ, no meaningful relationship to him. I had nothing I wanted to pass on to my own kids.

That night, I felt a driving hunger to find out what was true, to search for something real, something I could believe in and give my life to. In the weeks and months that followed, two thoughts broke into my mind again and again, both about Mother and Dad.

The first one was this: *They never gave up on me.* I gave them plenty of reason to do so with years of rebellion against their standards and a thoroughly selfish determination to get what I wanted out of life. I gave Mom and Dad some really hard times, but I never felt they rejected me. Their love for me outlasted the pain I caused them. They got mad at me, sometimes disgusted, but they never resented me. They never gave up.

The second thought is just as clear: *They are committed to Christ.* And this commitment is central, stronger even than their commitment to me. Someone was a bigger part of their life than I was, and somehow that fact enabled them to keep me as a painful part. I knew that no matter what I did, they would keep on following Christ. I didn't have the power to get them to give up on me or to stop serving Christ.

Those two thoughts reached deep within me. I now believe that God used my parents' refusal to back away from me to arouse my thirst for grace. And he used their unbendable commitment to Christ to persuade me that there was something bigger than me worth living for.

Whether I was converted in my thirties or came back to Christ then, I really don't know. But, as I've heard Dad say so often, the only real question is, What am I depending on right now for eternal life? And I know my answer is the finished work of Christ.

I suppose we all scream at God at times, reminding him of things for which we think he ought to repent. The two memorial services for Bill made it clear that God had used my brother in powerful ways in many people's lives. But couldn't God have gotten more mileage out of Bill by giving him another twenty years?

And the anguish for Phoebe: is anything worse than a widow's grief? Bill's two children, now young adults, no longer have the father who had so much to tell them about believing and living.

My parents, both in their seventies when Bill died, were rocked by his death as nothing else had rocked them in all their years. And I instantly became an only child who had lost a good brother and a close friend.

Sometimes I shake my head and cry, "Bill, I wish you were here. God, why did you take him?" But the weight of neither Dad's urging nor mine can persuade God to repent. And for a simple reason. He has made no mistake.

As I read how my father handled the death of his older son, I'm helped by realizing that our reactions are not always pretty. But if they're honest and if we yield to that quiet witness that God is still good, then God will carry us through the darkest valleys of life. He will never give up on us, and he is committed to a plan far larger than we can see, a plan that, one day we will agree, is wonderful. ❧

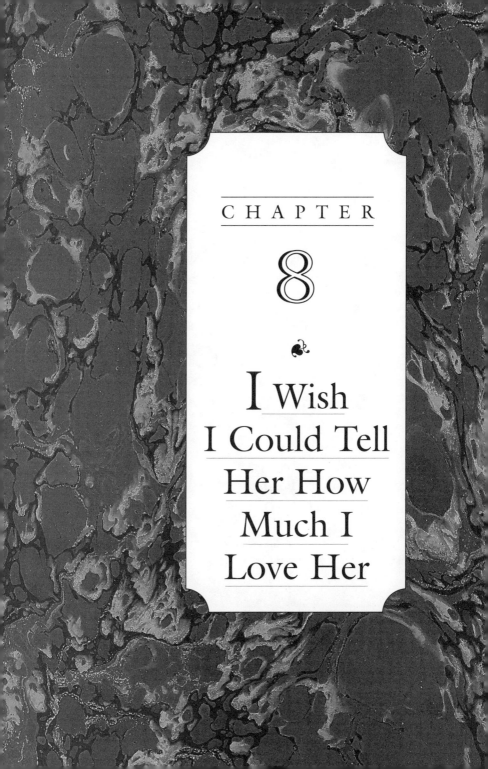

CHAPTER

8

I Wish
I Could Tell
Her How
Much I
Love Her

Dad and Mother a year before they
got married, spring 1937

Sixty queens there may be, . . .
but my dove, my perfect one,
is unique.

SONG OF SOLOMON 6:8–9

A Father's Recollections . . .

I write this late at night. My wife, Isabel, is napping on the sofa in our living room while I have been reading in a nearby chair. The book drops to the floor as an old love song plays through my mind:

> *I've known all its weariness, its pain and its*
> *   fears*
> *But its moments of happiness are worth all its*
> *   tears.*

I find myself looking at this woman, one who is so much a part of me. We are actually one flesh, something God has joined together.

Can it be fifty-two years since we said, "I do"? I'm too sleepy for exact calculations, but it's now 1990, so my figures must be fairly accurate.

It all started when I was a sophisticated twenty-one-year-old. Who can argue with maturity? "We five" were still very much together, still living at the Baynton Street home, still attending the Germantown Gospel

Hall, although it was now in a new building. One Sunday morning I looked around and noticed a new family. Three girls!

The service ended, and I began my usual chore of picking up the hymnbooks. My territory was the right-hand aisles. Somehow I traded with Al, who was in charge of the center aisles, the territory that included the row where the girls were sitting. Feeling as if I were the master of repartee, I ventured a timid hello and gained an interested nod from the one that mattered, the oldest, Isabel.

Things really developed from that point. I had taken permanent responsibility for the row where we had first met, and my "Hello" grew into some truly brilliant conversation. "Nice day."

"Sure is."

"Do you live nearby?"

"Not too far."

It's wonderful how such nothings can become so meaningful.

Then I unexpectedly met Isabel in Snellenbergs' department store in central Philadelphia. Much later she told me that she had been shopping for some feminine articles that would have been embarrassing for male eyes. Instead of continuing to shop, she told me she hadn't found what she needed.

I, of course, had completely forgotten why I was in town. We traveled back to her home by trolley and subway. I still recall checking my wallet and grandly pulling out a one dollar bill (my one and only) and paying both fares. I was nonchalant, unflappable in the face of financial ruin. I did consider stopping for a soda at one of the drug stores we passed, but since I had enough money for only one soda, I resolutely resisted temptation.

It was still the Depression, a long down period beginning with the stock-market crash of 1929. My job with the Philadelphia branch of the Maytag Company earned me very little money, but it was major help in providing for our family. After my brother, Cecil, married and moved out of the house, I was the only wage-earner.

After I left Maytag, I began my own business, an appliance sales and service store in Cortland, New York. Two years later, debt free, I came back to Philadelphia. Isabel was still waiting.

I found a position with the local branch of a company then known as Skilsaw (now Skil Corp.). I finally felt it was time to propose to Isabel and write her parents for permission to marry her. We couldn't get married right away because my financial prospects were bleak. But after her parents gave us their approval, I bought the engagement ring. Putting it on her finger was really something. And I chose a private place for this event: the rumble seat of my brother's car.

We later had a simple wedding held in Isabel's living room. The preacher was Harold Harper, the man who challenged me to give my life to the Lord. At my request, he asked only questions answerable by two-word answers. That's all the speaking I was capable of handling. I remember very little of the ceremony: saying "I do," putting the ring on my new wife's finger, hearing Harold Harper say, "I now pronounce you man and wife," and the well-wishing of our families and friends. I remember it only through a fog.

As I think back, I recall an uneasy realization of the once-for-allness of those words: "I now pronounce you man and wife." Oh, I would do it again. The decision was not impulsive, not after a courtship of over five years. The uneasiness had nothing to do with any reluctance either of us felt. We were just facing the grim economic realities that would hit us after the honeymoon.

"Man and wife." A permanent oneness. We had talked of it so many times. Ours would be a marriage of sharing: one bank account, no "his" and "her" distinctions. Never for a moment have I regretted this union, but the meaning of what I was doing pressed on me in those moments so many years ago. I had long ago committed this to the Lord, but now he seemed to be speaking so distinctly, so searchingly of his thoughts on this new relationship. "Husbands, love your wives, even as Christ also loved the church, and gave himself for it" (Eph. 5:25 KJV). When God looks at marriage, he sees a picture of Christ and his bride, the church. I knew I would mar the picture.

As I now watch Isabel sleeping on the sofa, I think of the first time I kissed her. I had driven her home from some event and was just about to say the usual goodnight when a daring thought entered my mind. This was still early in our courtship, but so many of my friends had bragged of a kiss on their first date. First date? What was wrong with me? I took a deep breath and then asked, "May I kiss you goodnight?" She made no response. Maybe she hadn't heard me. It was now or never, a major milestone. Then she looked up, and I almost ruined it. Was this a yes? I wasn't sure. I decided to kiss her and find out. It was the longest and shortest goodnight kiss I can remember.

Somewhere I read that "only God can be known as an increasingly pleasurable experience. To know any other well is a mixture of emotions from fulfillment to disappointment." Not even the most happily married man on earth can deny the sorrow of that fact, but truly love's "moments of happiness are worth all its tears."

Songs, poetry, the language of love, always belong in marriage. But we should not indulge a tendency to overpaint or to speak in idyllic terms. "We've never had a cross word between us; ours has been uninterrupted bliss." Such glowings I find hard to believe.

Our marriage, truly a good one, has survived misunderstandings, tears, and words spoken with the intent to hurt. But who can know the intense wonder of reconciliation without knowing what makes it necessary?

Did we ever have thoughts of separation or divorce? Did we contemplate the easy way out: "You go your way; I'll go mine"? Never.

When I spoke earlier of "never for a moment regretting this union," I meant every word. We certainly had moments of anger or impatience, but I don't remember ever thinking our marriage was a mistake or that I could possibly have married the wrong person. If someone had asked either of us, even under stress of battle, "Would you again take this woman; would you again take this man?" we would have had only one answer: "Of course! We're in love."

What does it mean to be in love? It's a striking phrase. To be in love is to be immersed in, surrounded by the most powerful of emotions. To be in love is to partake of the very essence of God. "God *is* love" (1 John 4:8).

But beyond that we are in love, "in Christ." "In Christ" is not an empty phrase: every believer is immersed in and surrounded by the One who somehow compressed himself in human form. And then take it even another step: *in love, in Christ, in God.* "For . . . your life is hid with Christ in God" (Col. 3:3 KJV). That's the full package.

The awesome wonder of all that it means to be in love, in Christ, in God is associated with the highest of earthly relationships: marriage. Paul speaks of marriage as a mystery, likening it to the oneness of Christ and his church (Eph. 5:32).

Marriage is a picture of something more than it ever captures, a union that speaks of a oneness yet to be known. What draws a man to a woman, a woman to a man? Surely the foundation of the deep love necessary for marriage is participation in the very essence of God. We all bear his image. We are the relational creation of a relational Being.

What draws us together goes far beyond any virtue, physical beauty, or abilities. It goes far beyond Samson's shallow motives when he ordered his parents, "Get that woman; she pleases me." (Judg. 14) His "pleasure" in the woman hardly made him a desirable life partner. The basis of a good marriage goes far beyond pleasure. To say she pleases me, get her for me, is to say, "She'll do fine as long as she gives me pleasure."

The divine pattern for marriage—Christ and his bride—reaches deeper into our souls. Christ loved the church and gave himself for it. Christ set the pattern for other-centeredness, a radical passionate commitment to devote all our resources to the welfare of the person we love.

The essence of a good marriage, of two becoming one flesh, is from above. Isabel and I are *in love, in Christ, in God.*

I'm still looking at my sleeping wife. I wish I could tell her how much I love her. Oh, I've tried, but words are such poor vehicles. The old song, true of my father, is equally true of me:

> *I plan such pretty speeches,*
> *Whenever we're apart,*
> *But when you're near, the words I choose*
> *Refuse to leave my heart.*
>
> *So take the sweetest phrases,*
> *The world has ever known*
> *And make believe*
> *I've said them all to you.*

I love you, Isabel.

A Son's Reflections . . .

My father is a passionate man. Writing this book together has given me a clearer glimpse into his passion than all the other opportunities I've had to know him. As with most men, expressing his deepest feelings does not come naturally. But the feelings are there. For him, it is easier to write what he feels than to say it.

My reluctance to express certain things takes a somewhat different form. I can more fully reveal my heart to an audience than to one person. The eye contact of a crowd seems far less intense than the stare of one person. Needless to say, this particular combination of relational dynamics in Dad and me does not encourage certain kinds of spoken communication between us.

A few years ago, we were walking together through a magnificent mountain gorge. The setting begged for rich conversation.

We had just listened to a mutual friend tell the story of his very difficult journey through personal crises toward maturity. It was a moving talk. At least it should have been. He had spoken with obvious passion, but his presentation lacked something. Even though I knew the man well and had walked with him on part of his journey, I had not been terribly stirred during his presentation.

As Dad and I stopped next to a fast-flowing mountain stream, I said, "That was quite a talk, wasn't it. He really held nothing back. But I was surprised by how little it moved me. I wanted to feel more than I did. But I still appreciated how open he was about his own life and about what he deeply felt."

I continued, a bit hesitantly, "You know, I sometimes wonder if we express ourselves in our family as openly as we should. I know that we have very rich feelings for each other, but we don't often put them into words."

Dad didn't respond. His face assumed that familiar I'm-thinking-hard look. After a few seconds, he replied,

"Don't you think that people today try to put too many of their emotions into words? I sometimes wonder if they are trying to create what they want to feel but don't."

He paused, then added, "The deepest bond between two people really can't be expressed in words."

My father enjoys dialogue. He rarely demands agreement, but I find I usually agree with him. I respect his wisdom. I don't disagree lightly.

But in this matter of expressing feelings, I have a different slant. When I have his years under my belt, I may eat my words, but I envision a healthy midpoint between too much expression and too little. His generation, I suspect, didn't say enough. Mine says too much. In marriage especially, we need to avoid both extremes and find that midpoint.

But that midpoint is hard to define. Is it different for different generations? Have Rachael and I more fully expressed our longings, joys, and conflicts to one another than Mother and Dad have to each other in their half-century of marriage? And if so, has it been good, or have we simply given in to the faddish wisdom of modern psychology?

Does each couple need to find its own midpoint, perhaps different in each case, depending on culture and generation? Or is there a norm of openness that marriage partners should move toward? The couples whose level of intimacy seems enviable to me have been drawn together more often, I think, by profound kindness, shared hardships, and individual maturity than by courageous vulnerability or aggressive sharing.

Knowing God well enough to be like him seems more important than expressing emotion. But openness, like disrobing, does have a place in marriage.

This morning I went to the cardiologist to walk a treadmill. A few troubling symptoms—chest pain, left-arm discomfort, unusual fatigue—had persuaded my physician to recommend a closer look at my heart. We expected good news, but we also knew there were no guarantees. I was apprehensive. I'm at the right age and stress level for a heart attack.

As I dressed to leave home for the test, I became aware of how much I wanted Rachael to come with me. If I was about to hear bad news, I wanted *her* with me, no one else.

But I hesitated in telling her what I wanted. Why? Was I afraid she would refuse to come or perhaps come grudgingly? Do I hate to appear needy? Did I feel like a child asking Mother to hold his hand while the mean doctor stuck his arm with a needle?

I decided this was a time to express my desire: to say what I meant, to admit what I wanted, and to express how badly I wanted it. So I summoned the necessary courage and said, "I really would like you to come with me to the clinic for this test."

Rachael immediately bounced out of bed and replied, "I'll be ready in five minutes." Later that morning, the doctor diagnosed a healthy heart; I emerged from the testing room, a little sweaty but flashing the thumbs-up sign to my eagerly waiting wife. That moment meant something to me, something rich. We exchanged no words, just a deep understanding.

Togetherness during important times reaches deep. And cultivating the best kind of togetherness requires that we become aware of our desires and express them to each other. We must not demand a response, but still we should clearly state our personal wants.

We not only need to express our desires, but we also need to express a second passion: joy. That joy is not the mere lightheartedness that leads to pleasant banter or the frivolous giddiness that modern church music sometimes reflects, but *joy*, that quiet, invincible sense of cheer that comes from knowing our Lord has overcome the world. Real joy belongs to community. It should be shared. But it is more difficult for me to tell my wife when I feel really good than when I feel bad.

Recently, I made a tough decision that was long overdue. I finally made it when I realized that not making it would rob me of involvement in something God was doing. The decision lifted me anew into God's larger story and filled me with joy. I sensed a burden lifted. Peace replaced turmoil and allowed me to sleep well, something I rarely do.

The next morning I awoke feeling refreshed and rested. I felt good enough to belt out a few tunes while I showered. My wife heard the noise. (She had little choice.) When I entered the bedroom with a towel wrapped around my waist, she commented, "Sounds as if you slept pretty well."

Immediately, something that had been dancing inside me slowed down. The words that climbed naturally up my throat were, "Oh, not bad. Better than usual, I guess."

But that wasn't true. I hadn't slept merely better than usual; I had slept *great!* Why didn't I easily say so? Do I like keeping the focus on me as a burdened, weary struggler? Do I want her to keep worrying about me?

Or am I afraid she will presume on my energy and expect me to feel good all day?

I really don't know why it would have been easier to say "not bad," but I believe we need to express the passion of joy when we feel it. I summoned my courage and told her the truth: "Honey, I slept great. I feel really good." She beamed. I wish I gave her more opportunities to share my joy.

A third passion I think we should express is the passion of struggle. Every marriage has a few "theme complaints," a relational pattern that pops up repeatedly and creates significant tensions. Rachael and I recognize one of our theme complaints: we don't often express our disappointments in each other without seeming to attack or without the listener feeling pressured to respond well.

Why do we so easily feel assaulted? Since Rachael and I married each other, we have never regretted getting married and we have never wanted anyone else for a spouse. Why, then, do the struggles continue?

I don't know, and I don't expect to figure it all out. But I do know that neither of us likes conflict. We are tempted, therefore, to keep our frustrations and problems to ourselves. Why risk a fight? It's simply easier to avoid talking about certain things.

But then we feel distant from one another, sometimes resentful: "If I can't talk with my own spouse about my troubles, whom can I talk to?"

Through our twenty-seven years of marriage, we're learning to overlook concerns that in earlier days we would heatedly discuss. We are discovering that as love matures, it covers a larger multitude of sins.

But our longing to enjoy each other sometimes provokes us to bring up hard issues that we know stand between us. I'm glad, because when people don't communicate, they assume the worst. And, if the worst is true, they know it's bad enough to threaten the continued existence of the relationship.

Then bad logic takes over. If people value the relationship and can't bear the thought of losing it, they are terrified to admit that something lethal might be wrong. So they back away from an honest exposure of what is in each other's hearts and never discover that beneath the conflict burns a love that could restore the warmth. Or, if the worst is true, they never find out that the relationship has died, and they continue in an empty marriage that honors no one rather than doing everything they can to build a better marriage.

Every time Rachael and I survive one of our low times, we realize a little more how deeply we do love each other. Bringing up the tough stuff forces us to fall back on our commitment to hang in there until death do us part. It requires us to pull out of our stubborn hearts the love that God has placed there. The effect has been, after enduring more pain than either of us cares to remember, the emergence of a sturdy togetherness that we know can survive whatever storms lie ahead. Expressing the passion of struggle is sometimes the right thing to do.

When I express any one of these three passions— desire, joy, or struggle—something inside me is threatened. Learning to express these passions without demanding a response, without worrying whether the joy will last, and without creating pressure in my wife to handle me well is a continuing process. But *not* expressing these passions creates a barrier to intimacy. Something is left in place, and that barrier comes between us. For my part, I would rather endure discomfort that leads to closeness than avoid it and remain distant.

But intimacy does not depend on improved communication. My father has taught me that the richest intimacy between a man and woman grows out of something far more sublime than sharing feelings. The best marriage depends on a relationship with God through Christ, a relationship that frees us to love for a lifetime and to get better at it as we go along.

Rachael and I have weathered a few storms that good communication could never have handled. Many of our battles were resolved through expressing ourselves with honesty and respect, but the big ones required more.

Dad spoke of "words intended to hurt." Did he mean that? Is he a man like me, with a heart capable of *wanting* to hurt the woman he loves most in all the world? How can anyone become intimate with someone who occasionally tries to harm you? Rachael and I have never hurt anyone else so badly or so meanly as we have each other. But we're still together, and, like Mother and Dad, we're deeply in love. How can this be?

Sometimes I watch Rachael talking to a friend with lively animation or driving off waving a cheery good-bye or simply lying in bed, and I feel something, something I feel for no one else, something I could never put into words. And I know that the source of my emotion goes beyond all that I find attractive in her. I sense that I am with her, walking together along a difficult but good path that leads to fulfilled desire, eternal joy, and total freedom from conflict. In that day, we'll have no trouble expressing the passions we will feel.

Rachael is my partner in a high calling. When I catch even a glimpse of what it means to be *in love, in Christ, in God,* it takes my breath away. The reality is so much bigger than all our fears and failures and attacks and insecurities.

They say imitation is the sincerest form of flattery. If that is so, then my parents are in danger of developing oversized heads. I have learned from them, as Rachael has learned from her parents, to build our marriage on a foundation stronger than shared feelings, open communication, or natural affection. We are in love, in Christ, in God. It sometimes leaves me speechless. I wish I could tell her how much I love her, but the deepest bond between two people really can't be expressed in words. 🕭

CHAPTER

9

❧

Will I
Be
Missed?

Dad at his eightieth birthday party, 1992

I have fought a good fight,
I have finished my course,
I have kept the faith.
2 TIMOTHY 4:7 KJV
But I fear that I may have "run
in vain."
GALATIANS 2:2 KJV

A Father's Recollections . . .

Will I be missed when I die?

It's three o'clock in the morning, hardly an auspicious time to resolve this question. Frankly I have a tendency to avoid serious thought along these lines, but a pamphlet lying here compels more than light meditation.

In Memory
of
Dr. William T. Crabb
1940–1991

I find it very difficult to write about this. I can more easily accept the death of older people, but this—this was a stab aimed directly at the heart. Bill had been a young man. It seems as if it was only a few months ago that I went with him to the Air Force Academy where he had passed a grueling physical with flying colors. Having retired from the Air Force, he was involved in a second career, a new ministry as a biblical counselor.

I knew Bill's life counted for something, but I never realized the deep impact his life had made on others until I attended the two memorial services, one in Colorado and the other in South Carolina. Both were moving testimonials to his understanding and compassion in touching people's lives. Between these two services, the Air Force conducted an honor-guard service in South Carolina.

The three events over a period of less than a week were emotionally draining. I think of Bill's wife, his son, his daughter, his brother, his mother, and so many others who deeply miss him. A literal flood of letters arrived after Bill's death. One person said of him, "Bill went home to glory. The angels are singing."

Another person reflected, "Jesus is in the business of reconciliation, and Bill was doing his Savior's business. Bill's deeds will be remembered because they were corporate resolutions in the company of Christ."

Others rejoiced, "How we thank God for Bill and his life, for his gentle and sensitive spirit, for his openness about his own personal struggles. He touched many, many lives and was used by the Lord to bring healing and change in many. We loved him as a friend and brother."

Another friend thought about Bill in heaven and wrote to Larry, Jr., "I was listening to your father's last 'elder chat' when he spoke of getting a whiff of eternity as he grew older. I'm sure the whiff will be even stronger with a son there. I thank God for Bill's ministry."

At the memorial services many people expressed their gratitude for Bill's counsel in their lives. It was a revelation to Isabel and me. We knew Bill had been doing counseling, but because of the confidentiality he granted to each person, we had never questioned him about his work and he had never volunteered more than superficial information.

But no one held anything back at either of the gatherings, as men and women told, many with tears, of the way Bill had affected their lives. One young woman whom we knew well compared herself to Lazarus and said Bill's understanding and constant pointing to Christ had brought her back to life.

When I think of the people's responses at Bill's memorial services, I wonder if I will be missed when I die. Is this even a legitimate question? Does it reflect a violation of Paul's instructions that we should do everything to the glory of God (1 Cor. 10:31)? Am I really more concerned with *my* glory than God's? Where do I go for answers? The safe people, those who are close friends, would certainly say that they will miss me. But what about others?

I don't want to be like King Jehoram, "Thirty and two years old was he . . . and departed without being desired" (2 Chron. 21:20). Frankly, he died unmourned.

Oh, I know people will mourn. But I want something more. Will I be missed as Bill is missed?

Should I *prepare* to be missed? Do I want to be missed more than others who have already died? Am I to spend the rest of my life ensuring that a stream of testimonials will flow from my death?

Some people will be missed more than others. To make "being missed" a goal invites a selfish obsession.

Did Bill ever give the slightest thought to whether lots of people would come to his memorial services? Surely not! And therein lies the secret of a life that is pleasing to God.

On the one hand, to *prepare* to be missed is, I am convinced, a self-seeking occupation. On the other hand (I assume my readers are hanging on every word as maturity speaks with such dogmatic hesitancy), it's important to build up personal relationships that will result in our being missed.

Each "missing" is intensely individual; sorrow, like joy, is personal. How I miss my mother, my son, my sister, my brother, and my father, even though I knew him for so short a time.

I certainly share my sorrow with other people; Isabel and our family often share memories of Bill. But the richest sorrow is the kind I feel when I am alone with God and I talk to him about Bill. I find that missing Bill is a unique hurt that will never go away until I see him again. But even through tears I thank God for so many times we experienced a oneness. I mattered to Bill, and he mattered to me.

Four days have passed since I wrote the preceding pages. As I reread them I again have the sense of disputable finality, a sense of painting myself into a corner. Yes, I want to be missed, ego trip or no. A death like King Jehoram's makes me shudder. On the other hand, I want no part of planning to make my death a tragic loss.

The solution is that God must be the great Initiator in any course of action that will make me worthy of being truly missed. Paul told us, "Work out your own salvation in fear and trembling. For *it is God which worketh in you* both to will and to do of his good pleasure" (Phil. 2:12–13, emphasis added KJV). It is only as God works in me that I can will and do of his good pleasure. My only legitimate goal is his good pleasure, not whether people will miss me.

Will I be missed? Yes, but only to the degree that other people have seen Christ in me. Paul longed that God might "reveal his Son" in him (Gal. 1:16 KJV). Note the beautiful sequence here. God reveals himself *in his Son,* then reveals himself *in us* as we allow him to work "both to will and to do of his good pleasure." To make a difference in even one life, to be a part of that divine sequence as God reveals his Son in me guarantees that I will be missed, although being missed is not my purpose in life.

The people whom we really miss are those who, like Bill, have left a continuing fragrance. "Precious in the sight of the LORD [and to us] is the death of his saints" (Ps. 116:15).

Will I be missed? That is not the crucial issue. The most important issue is the realization that Christ has abolished death and brought us eternal life and immortality in a world beyond our world of questions and sorrow.

My papa knew that when he died. That realization allowed him to comfort my mother with his confident, "Hush! God is in it." Have I fully entered into the calm my papa knew? I have only fleeting whiffs from the land beyond. Lord, send me another whiff, please!

Even as I cry, the Lord answers with a story I deeply love. A distraught man tearfully implores the

Lord: "My son is dying. If you can do anything, please help us."

The Lord replies, "If you can believe, all things are possible."

With grim honesty the poor man answers, "Lord, I believe. Help my unbelief" (Crabb's translation of Mark 9).

What sort of belief is this? How can the Lord respond to what amounts to, "I believe. At least I *believe* I believe. Help me!" Surely the Lord must turn away from such anemic trust. But according to the story, the Lord responds to this cry so lacking in conviction, so wanting in confidence, falling so far short of his condition: "If you can believe."

Yes, I still want to be missed when I die, but more importantly I want to walk close to the Lord, share his thinking, and become like him. When someone is like him, that person always leaves a lasting fragrance that other people will miss.

A Son's Reflections . . .

I don't like thinking about my father's death. I'll miss him, terribly. But sometimes it's harder to think about his life. What I know about my father's experience of God and of himself has severely disrupted my comfortable ideas about Christianity.

Perhaps I'm wrong to be so disrupted. Maybe Dad is really an immature man whom I shouldn't take so seriously. After all, even though Dad has lived over eighty years, all of them among Christians, most of them as a Christian, he has not fully developed into the kind of man I always assumed I would one day become. Perhaps I need to learn about God and maturity from other sources.

I wish he spoke more often in glowing terms of the Spirit's provision of boundless joy. I wish he delighted in the powerful certainty of revealed truth so that he no longer wrestled with confusion and doubt. I wish he could report that opportunities for meaningful ministry are wonderfully compensating for the pleasures lost to old age.

Instead, he tells me that God never showed up during his worst moments after open heart surgery. In those ten days of recovery in the hospital, he never felt the inspiring closeness with Christ, as everyone supposes mature Christians feel when life leads them through dark valleys. When I look at my dad's life, I ask myself, Will God show up when I suffer?

Instead, his dreams for retirement—sharing in the work of a local church, dialoguing with like-minded Christians about the rich things of Christ, enjoying retreats with his two sons, their wives, and children— have not come true. Some have been utterly shattered. I have dreams too. What will happen to them?

Instead, he worries about whether people will miss him after he dies, and he worries about it during his firstborn son's memorial service. Is that commendable? Is that part of maturity? Crazy thoughts run through my mind too, often at the least appropriate times. But I thought things might be different when I got to be his age.

What do I have to look forward to? What does maturity look like? Paul's words strike terror into my heart: "If only for this life we have hope in Christ, we are to be pitied more than all men" (1 Cor. 15:19). Does that mean that the only guaranteed relief from misery is our hope for another world? What blessings can I depend on now from the hand of God:

- the comfort of his presence in a hospital room?
- doing something that feels important until the day I die?
- good friends who always arrive when I feel lonely?
- maturity that excites me with how much I am coming to resemble Christ?
- noble impulses replacing base ones?
- internal energy that makes other-centeredness more natural and less of a disciplined choice?

Is it really possible that *none* of these blessings is guaranteed? Must I live with no other anchor than the declared character of God, and must I cling to that truth when my experience of life provides no support for faith?

A father is one who travels ahead on a path he invites his son to walk. As I watch my father from thirty years behind, I think I hear him say, "Follow me as I follow Christ. But get ready to be surprised. The path of pursuing God is very different from what you expect. At least it has been for me."

Godly mentors disrupt their students. Perhaps that's the major value of a mentor, to lead a life that cannot be easily explained, a life that makes no sense to earth-bound thinking, a life that to most people is unattractive. My father has disrupted my understanding of many things, but two stand out above the rest: the character of God and the nature of maturity. A few comments on each will indicate how severe—and I hope productive—the disruption has been.

First, my father has disrupted my understanding of the character of God. Ever since I was a child, I've wanted to know God. I knew Christianity was more than enjoying youth group hay rides that began with the required prayer and ended with a sobering devotional that seemed intended to keep us from having too much fun. The point of the evening for us was the good time in between. I liked the fun.

During those years, I was not known as a serious seeker. No one would have seen the hunger in my soul for the reality of God. It was there, but I hid it beneath convertibles, silliness, athletics, and popularity. No one asked me to give the closing devotional or lead the Bible study. People assumed I was content with the good things in my life.

But I knew there was more, and I wanted it. I wanted more than a fulfilling, interesting, enjoyable life sandwiched between opening prayers and closing devotionals. I wanted to know the God to whom we prayed and the God whom the devotional supposedly revealed.

From early days, my symbol of God was the sky. The sheer mystery of endless blue fascinated me. I recall when I first learned that each star was a huge chunk of matter bigger than the earth I lived on. Dozens of times, I would walk out the front door after sunset and lie down on my back on our front lawn. As I stared at the little white dots scattered across the dark sky, I pondered the idea that I could move into that sky for a million years and never bump into it. It went on forever. It was big.

More than once, I asked out loud if I could meet the Person who made it all.

Most adults who were in a position to introduce God to me tried to *explain* him: here's what he wants you to do; here's what he'll do if you obey him; here's what he'll do if you don't; here's how to be sure of heaven; here's how to read the book that makes everything clear. I remember thinking they were describing a divine Santa Claus who was less jolly than I wished and more committed to rule keeping than I could ever be but still someone who had a bag full of toys. God was too often presented as a wonderful treat available to those who figured out the system and played it well. I did not get the idea of God as an attractive mystery.

Except from Dad. I remember listening to him pray. His prayers struck me as different from those of the other men in our little church. Without working hard, I could anticipate the other men's phrases and silently mimic their inflections. When they prayed, it seemed more like bad theater than conversation with God. But when Dad prayed, I could tell he thought he was actually talking to Somebody.

Dad always used King James English when he prayed. But it never sounded artificial or strained. He once explained that he wanted to address God differently from how he addressed anyone else. I got the idea that, to him, God was a real person, too big to figure out but available enough to be known.

My first major faith crisis occurred when I left home for graduate school. I gave up whatever was left of my belief in an *explained* God to set out in search of the *mysterious* God, the God of my father. Perhaps the most significant discovery I made in the early days of my search was that God didn't play by the system I thought he made up. I could intentionally do something wrong one night and still score an *A* on the next day's exam. I began to see that sin doesn't always (at least not immediately) interfere with comfort but that it always hurts relationship.

Like every proud rationalist, I hate mystery. It leaves me so helpless, so dependent on someone I can neither predict nor control. I would rather cooperate with a reliable God than worship an unmanageable one. I therefore spent most of my twenties and thirties and half of my forties holding out for a not-quite-so-mysterious God. The passion to package God into someone who makes sense runs deep.

When a good friend read me a line in which novelist Annie Dillard called God a maniac, I was offended. He thought her description was intriguing. At that time, I did not yet realize an important truth: when the effort to reduce God into someone who can be understood and used is combined with the courage to face life honestly, God does look like a maniac, like a fickle tyrant who is benevolent one moment, indifferent the next, and sometimes downright cruel.

I have learned to appreciate my father's willingness to let God be the mystery that he is and, with eyes wide open, to pursue him, not with the precision of a crossword puzzle fanatic but with the reckless passion of a pilot flying into the Bermuda Triangle. Following Christ is a wild adventure full of risk, frustration, excitement, and setbacks. It is not an evening stroll in a planned community along a well-manicured path.

But following Christ is also not a foolish leap into darkness. Beneath my father's confusion, questions, and struggles is an anchor. He deeply believes God is good. The death of Christ, which he remembers every week in the Lord's Supper, is proof of that. Forsaking God is as unthinkable to Dad as divorcing my mother. Relationship defines the meaning of his existence. As I follow behind him, I'm learning that the path to God takes me beyond the classroom where I study his character and into the sanctuary where I enjoy his heart. Perhaps someday I'll experience God's unpredictability as delightful.

The second area of thinking that my father's life disrupts is my understanding of spiritual maturity. I still cling to the hope that one day before heaven I'll be able to look in the mirror and congratulate God on what a fine job he has done in remaking me. So far, I've been able to thank him only for continuing to put up with me.

But maybe that's the point: *maybe growth consists not in a sharper awareness of our maturity but in a puzzled appreciation of mercy.* God is still involved with me? He actually *delights* in me? Incredible! The leap from maturity to glorification is far greater, I suspect, than the distance from conversion to maturity.

Christian leaders too often present themselves as having the important things in their lives together. In many cases, job security depends on it. The struggles they share are usually reported in the past tense. "I don't mind admitting to you that I once had a real problem with this or that, but God in his marvelous grace has taken it away." The clear message is that those of us still struggling with this or that are lagging behind on the road to maturity.

But the Bible paints a disturbing portrait of its heroes, a portrait that doesn't match the picture of problem-free maturity. Moses hit a rock; David stole a woman; Jonah got mad when his enemies turned to God; Elijah wished to die; Jeremiah called God a dried-up brook; Paul felt soul-crushing loneliness; Peter was snobbish at a dinner party. These people give me hope.

Perhaps maturity does not mean the end of struggle and failure so much as the *courage to move through them*. Maturity might even involve the deepening of problems. Petty complaint sometimes matures into shattering discouragement. Immoral behavior yields to a relentless battle against twisted desires. Naïve optimism gives way to realistic despair. Perseverance becomes a more cherished virtue than enjoyment.

By the standards of too many evangelicals, my father is not especially mature. His testimony does not include daily miracles and unremitting joy and constant excitement over meaningful ministry. Those standards make me want to give up. I don't expect ever to become down here the man I will be up there.

But perhaps, like Dad, I can be mature enough to enter into mystery, cling to what is clear, and continue yielding to the unquenchable passion within me to know God regardless of whatever other passions, good or bad, remain within me. The longing to be missed, even when it is felt during your son's funeral, is no violation of maturity; in fact, it is part of maturity, if it does not quench a deeper longing to be like Christ. ❧

CHAPTER

10

❧

The Best
Is Yet to
Come

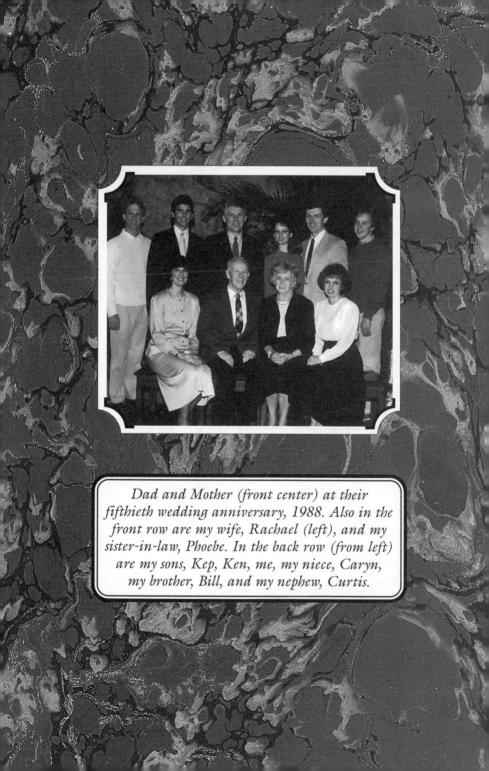

Dad and Mother (front center) at their fifthieth wedding anniversary, 1988. Also in the front row are my wife, Rachael (left), and my sister-in-law, Phoebe. In the back row (from left) are my sons, Kep, Ken, me, my niece, Caryn, my brother, Bill, and my nephew, Curtis.

No eye has seen, no ear has heard,
no mind has conceived
what God has prepared for those
who love him.
                                    1 CORINTHIANS 2:9

A Father's Recollections . . .

I remember the day so vividly. It was 1930, and I was eighteen. The evangelist was thundering, "Listen to me friends, and listen good! I accepted the Lord as my Savior on January 12, 1910, at high noon. Since that moment I have yet to experience the slightest shadow of doubt or uncertainty as to my salvation." Then he shouted, "God said it! I believe it! That settles it!"

"That's for me," I shouted inside. It sounded so majestically absolute, especially with the accompanying "Amens" and "Praise the Lords" from a rapt audience. I came to know the speaker fairly well and never saw in him evidence of anything but his dogmatic confidence; I wasn't particularly drawn to him. In his mind, the slightest doubt, the slightest deviation from a determined confidence was the unpardonable sin. I later came to see that pushiness as a stubborn refusal to think.

When I was younger, I wanted to be free from doubts and uncertainties. I wanted to know that I was saved. I wanted to be sure that God was watching over my family. I made the elimination of all uncertainty a goal. The problem is that assurance of salvation can easily become reliance on word repetition rather than on the finished work of Christ. I was substituting a formula for a person.

That longing for perfect peace has stayed with me. I want to receive the promise Isaiah outlined: "Thou wilt keep him in perfect peace, whose mind is stayed on thee: because he trusteth in thee" (Isa. 26:3 KJV). Peace, freedom from doubt, what a tremendous prospect. Will I ever know this?

I have yet to know, really know, someone who had the confident faith that preacher claimed to profess. Doubt is not the unpardonable sin. God knows what we are made of. He knows we are dust (Ps. 103:14). I don't believe our heavenly Father is offended by our questions. He gives "to all men liberally, and upbraideth not" (James 1:5 KJV).

I can't imagine my papa becoming impatient with sincere questions. When I was five years old, I saw him as an all-knowing one to whom I could come with the most unreasonable fears and questioning. He would give me understanding and help.

I would learn later that my papa had questions and doubts too. An old friend of his has told me of them. He and Papa had often talked long into the night with open Bibles, searching the Scriptures. The friend told me that Papa was unusual in that he admitted to fears that were simply not acceptable in evangelical circles, fears that he had the opportunity of talking about with this understanding friend.

I wish I could have talked with Papa about his questions—and my questions too, for that matter. I decided to write a letter to Papa, not for reassurance, but as an outlet.

Dear Papa,

I've wanted to do this for a long time. I know your address, but whether or not you'll ever read this is in the Lord's hands, his pierced hands. How fantastic it must be to be with the One who loved you and gave himself for you.

When you left us with "Hush, God is in it," there were Mother and the four children—we five. Now just Mabs and I are left here on earth. The family has expanded: Cecil had a boy; I have two boys (you've already met Bill); Helen had a boy; and Mabel had two girls.

I always think I have two families: the family into which I was born and the family that began when Isabel said, "Yes!" Mother told us of the time you introduced her to some friends with, "I know you'll like her. I do!" I can't wait to introduce you to Isabel: You'll like her. I do.

Papa, do you know that your little five-year-old Lawrence is now eighty? Do you ever think of yourself in earth years? You would be 106 years old. I don't think of you that way. I look at a photo on my desk and see a handsome, thirty-year-old man sitting on a wide chair with a charming woman standing behind him, both of her hands on his shoulders and a this-is-my-man smile on her face.

Mother aged; you stayed young. But now, what does it matter? What does anything matter? You're both with the Lord. All I remember of you is what a five-year-old sees. But, Papa, you left me good memories, memories that give me some concept of the One we both call Father, even to the point that I affectionately call him Papa.

We had so few years together. Oh, Papa. All of us knew you loved Mother, your Laura. And we knew you loved us. I remember family rules, rules that we sometimes broke and were disciplined for. But we always, always knew you would give us a smile and a hug. Do you remember taking your two boys for a train ride, patiently explaining to seven-year-old Cecil and me how steam was produced and made the wheels go around?

It won't be long now before the six of us are together again. If I had a choice, I would opt for the Rapture. Then we'll see each other as we were meant to be, not spirit beings as you are now, but with changed bodies, changed into his likeness.

You never knew old age. I wonder if Mother told you about it. I look at your photo—full head of hair, smooth skin, and although I can't see them, I'm sure you had all your teeth.

Keats spoke of staying forever young in his "Ode on a Grecian Urn," in which he depicts people in ageless frozenness, pursuing joy with no progress and no consummation. You know something far better, don't you, Papa? You know the fullness of joy in being in God's presence. I know this to a lesser extent, but still it's only a whiff of heaven. For you it's realization. For me it's only yearning.

Papa, your love for us made life far more than

mere existence. You had so little, yet you gave so much. How I wish I had known you better. I wish I could hear your footsteps on the stairs, to hear Mother's excited cry, "Papa's home!" Those words meant we were all together. We didn't comprehend it then, Papa, but you gave us all a whiff of heaven, the untroubled sense that all was well because Papa was home—and we were with him.

Again I look at the photo of you and Mother. The photo is very dear to me, but it's only paper. Will it soon be something like "a step on the stairs— Papa's home," as we meet to be forever together with the Lord?

Your son,

Lawrence

I had meant to ask Papa if he gave much thought to dying during his short life. Too late now. The letter was an indulgence, a reaching out to someone.

When I do see Papa, I really doubt if we will talk of his or my thoughts about death. Perhaps we'll talk over those earth days when we saw through a glass darkly, before we came face to face with the One who will then be part of our conversation. Our talk will not be like the conversation between the men on the road to Emmaus. What a tragedy. They knew who Christ was only as he left them. For Papa and me, and Bill and Mother, it will be so different. Imagine a Bible study led by the author.

These thoughts of Papa and heaven seem to catch me up into a vague world between heaven and earth. And yet a vision based on truth is more than a flight of wishful fancy. Could it be a foretaste of what our eyes have not yet seen and our ears have not yet heard, a glimpse of the things that God has prepared for them that love him (1 Cor. 2:9)?

The vision fades so easily in a world that is too much with us. This present world is tempting to all of us until things go wrong, until we find ourselves in want. Even then we still try the broken cisterns that hold no water (Jer. 2:13). When will we learn?

So many philosophers, psychologists, theologians, and poets brood about death. Shakespeare pessimistically wrote in *Macbeth:*

> *Life's but a walking shadow, a poor player*
> *That struts and frets his hour upon the stage*
> *And then is heard no more: It is a tale*
> *Told by an idiot, full of sound and fury,*
> *Signifying nothing.*

But their brooding seems little more than an effort to evade death's unbending finality.

We Christians speak happily, perhaps a bit glibly, about death. We fondly quote Paul's words of an instant, blessed change from here to there. All Scripture supports this assertion. And yet it is strikingly revealing that God in his infinite understanding of human weakness makes no attempt to minimize the reality that death is an enemy: "The last enemy that shall be destroyed is death" (1 Cor. 15:26 KJV).

Death is an enemy, the last enemy. And it will be destroyed.

Some, like the martyred Stephen, see through the shadows to the glory beyond, but I search in vain for a promise of a similar vision when I die. Will my death be like Christian's, the pilgrim in Bunyan's dream, who said as he died, "I sink in deep waters; all his waves go over me. I shall not see the land"? Or, will my death be more like Hopeful's, Christian's companion, who exulted, "I see the gate, and those standing by to receive us"?

Both got safely through; both were greeted with, "Enter ye into the joy of your Lord," but how different were their final moments. Both entered into oneness with the Warrior who abolished death: but to one, death was but a shadow; to the other, death was the last enemy.

I don't know how I will face my death. Still, I can speak sincerely of a whiff of heaven, a fragrance so intense, so inexpressibly captivating that it creates a longing for entrance into his presence, whether that entrance will be full of ease or plagued with doubting.

In the weariness of my eighty years, I sometimes find the words of Alexander Pope quite appealing, "Cease, fond nature, cease thy strife / And let me languish into life." But I find far more comfort in the words of the psalmist, "My times are in thy hand. . . . Oh how great is thy goodness" (Ps. 31:15–19 KJV).

Someday I'll hear the music clearly, the perfect harmony of fully restored relationships. Hints of that day are sprinkled throughout Scripture. During a time of celebration, Nehemiah wrote, "The singers sang loud, with Jezrahiah their overseer" (Neh. 12:42). Jezrahiah means "Jehovah shines forth." The picture of richer truth is incredibly charming. Jehovah, God himself, will one day be fully revealed, shining forth in his Son, who leads the innumerable choir of the redeemed. The rejoicing in heaven over one sinner who repents will soon reach its ultimate crescendo as all his redeemed enter into the fullness of his presence.

Now we catch an occasional whiff of heaven. Now we occasionally hear the distant harmony. But soon, we will smell the full aroma and hear the complete choir, with no one missing. So shall we ever be with the Lord.

A Son's Reflections . . .

I am in the perfect position to reflect on the past and anticipate the future. More than half my life is over, and, if you date the season of adult productivity from age twenty-five until incapacity or death, about half my ministry still lies ahead. From this high point, I can see a long way into the horizon on both sides. It's a good place, I am finding, to be captured by the drama of the larger story into which my life fits.

When I turn and look backward, I see two grandfathers, one who died twenty-seven years before I was born, the other a man I heard pray in an awestruck voice that told me he was in the presence of absolute majesty. He died when I was a teenager. Both were strong men of God.

I see two grandmothers, one who died a blind widow with the word "Hush" on her lips, the other a wonderfully traditional grandma who busily fussed over her young grandson. I remember early summer mornings on her porch on Penn Street, sipping ice water from a glass she faithfully kept filled, enjoying her appreciation of the colorful azaleas and fragrant lilacs.

If I squint my eyes enough to look even farther in the past, I can see five generations—perhaps there are more beyond my sight—of godly people from England on Dad's side, from Scotland on Mother's. Refocusing on more recent days brings into view involved parents who laughed, spanked, prayed, and served; a brother who was (and still is) bonded to me as no other man is; a pretty girl I met at age ten and married eleven years later; and two sons who were once little boys.

It's good to look to the past. Despite the troubles and heartaches that nostalgia cannot erase, the story of the past is reassuring. We can't change these chapters, and because they stand still, we can study them.

My past helps me believe in a larger story of which every detail I remember is merely a part. The many people and influences that make up my past do not strike me as a disconnected group of short stories; they rather seem like a few paragraphs in a very long novel that turns out to be true. The effect of reflecting on my history, and especially on the God of my father, is to strengthen the conviction that my life is part of a larger story, a story that is continuing through me and on beyond me through my sons. I can't express how much I enjoy that last thought!

The heights of middle age, to which I've ascended and from which I'll descend, have given me a clearer glimpse of the larger story that God began telling at the Fall and will keep telling until his Coming. We all know God is a master storyteller, but we often want him to direct his creative talents to a script we write. But he will have none of that. He insists on writing, producing, directing, casting, and starring in the eternal drama. He shares with his friends the central plot; he tells them what parts they can play. Then he invites them to assemble on the cosmic stage to enter the play, without audition or practice.

We never quite know how our few lines move the story along, but two things quickly become clear: one, none of us is the hero of the drama; and two, each of our roles, properly played, is taxing—following the script means giving up our comfort. We flub our lines regularly, but the director never loses patience. He doesn't seem to mind the endless retakes. All that matters is that we not quit.

As we get into the story, something strange happens. We begin to sense that the play is real life, and the life we live off stage is the shadow. And it becomes clear that the intended purpose in every chapter is to reveal that God is really good. Since Adam's sin, all his descendants have been living in the foggy world of doubt and suspicion. "Maybe God is not all that good; after all, look what he allowed to happen to me." Every part in the play contributes to the single purpose of dispelling the fog with the dazzling sunshine of God's revealed character.

The director gives to each of his children a part written precisely to match the person's background, circumstances, and talent. When I reflect on my past, I can see how so many people have played their part well. When I look to the future, I realize how much I want future generations to say the same thing of me. And I realize how passionately I long to see my sons play their parts well.

This book is about mentoring, about one generation of people passing on their faith to the next. As I end these reflections on my father's walk with God, I want to turn from looking at the past to looking at my sons' future. I want to encourage them to walk the path, to play their part, to see their lives as part of God's larger story. My heart beats fast and my eyes moisten as I write this letter to my sons.

Dear Kep and Ken,

I've never told you completely how much you mean to me because I can't. As my dad would say, the deepest bonds cannot be expressed in words. Through your mother, I have passed the miracle of life on to you. You are both fully individuals, unique and separate, but you are also extensions of the life that my father passed on to me and his father to him.

I remember, as if it were yesterday, staring at each of you in your cribs, many times crying. As I would kneel with tears of love and joy and hope pouring down my cheeks, I would lay my hand on you and pray, "God, make them yours! Remove the deception. Let them see how good you are. Give them your life—and may they give their lives to you."

I've been so scared. Sometimes my fears overcame my love and I lashed out at you; I demanded of you things that must come from your *own* desires and choices. I couldn't bear the thought of Satan winning in your lives. I was wrong to be so controlled by fear. God told me to rest, to trust him, and to believe in you. Instead, I sometimes took matters into my own hands, forgetting that only love, never pressure, draws people to God. Forgive me. Don't let it get in the way.

In your late teens and early twenties, I spent many nights in my study until the early morning, praying with more passion than I can describe. On so many occasions, my words, over and over, were, "Lord, give me my boys! Let me enjoy them as godly men!" I trembled before God, praying until I was too exhausted to say another word. I never heard God speak to me, but several times I sensed him smiling and saying, "Trust me."

I fear that I've given you the impression that godly living can be a rather joyless struggle. With all my heart, I wish I knew more of the joy that I'm convinced God intends us to know. My life has been—and still is—a battle. More than once, I've come close to quitting. Personal failures can seem overwhelming. Deep pain that I cannot explain is sometimes too much.

But I can't quit. I've tasted his grace. Every time I fail, I sense he is saying that he's not through with me. He forgives me and wants me to get up and get back on the path. And the pain, even at its worst, has never overcome my hope. I know that living now for Christ is worthwhile, despite the struggles, and that a better day—a *fantastic* day— is coming.

You're simply too young to think much of heaven. Death must seem far away to you. It did to me when I was your age. And it still seems far more remote to me than it does to my father.

But your uncle Bill's death has brought it closer. My dad's surgery has too. I've never before sensed the reality of Christ and the reality of heaven as I have these last several years. Can you imagine what heaven will be like? Think of your happiest moment ever, multiply it by ten thousand, then stretch it out to last forever. To be with someone who loves you perfectly and wants to share with you every pleasure that he can dream up—that's what lies ahead, more certainly than anything else you may anticipate.

I wish thoughts like that moved me more than they do. As I near age fifty, I'm aware of how *natural* a life I lead, but I'm more aware of how strenuously I long to lead a *supernatural* life. I sense God moving. Perhaps my favorite line in literature is C. S. Lewis's comment about the lion as Narnia's winter begins to break: "Aslan is on the move." I am thoroughly excited, and scared, about what lies ahead for me.

You are part of a story you never chose. All four of your grandparents, like all four of mine, love Jesus Christ. Both your parents love him. Our family is blessed beyond measure. And with blessing comes the responsibility of unique opportunity.

With the Christian legacy you've inherited from generations before you, you both have been prepared to live for him and to make a difference in this world. Leave your mark. Leave it on people: first on your wives, then on your children and friends. Don't look to do big things. Simply be faithful. Perhaps you will minister to thousands, maybe to only a handful. It really doesn't matter. Ask God to direct your steps faithfully into the part of his story he has already created for you.

There are no two men whom I love more than you two. Complete my joy by committing your lives to telling his story. Let your minds imagine the scene of your grandparents and mine, and theirs before them, gathering for a huge family reunion. Your uncle Bill will grab his guitar—he'll play it better then—Mother and I will smile at each other as we've never smiled before, Carolyn and Kim will be laughing and singing; and then we'll become quiet. The Lord will step into the middle of the circle and invite each of you to tell the story of how you lived for him on earth. You'll both burst with humble joy as you reflect on your decisions that honored the Savior; you'll slap each other on the back with excitement over how your lives counted. And when you finish your tale, the Lord will smile and with a tenderness that will forever amaze us all, will embrace you and say, "Well done. It's time for the party!"

Can you imagine watching my father dance? In ways that not even he understands, the best is yet to come.

Kep, I love you. Live for Christ.

Ken, I love you. Live for Christ.

Dad

A Note to the Reader

❧

I wonder what you feel now that you have read our book? Some of you may wonder if my sons will stagger under the weight of their blessing. I can only hope that they will be more enticed than pressured by all that has preceded them and remember that each person stands before God as an individual, alone in his or her story. As you read their responses to this book in the two sections that follow this note, you will see two young adult men in the process of finding the path.

Regardless of our background, we all need to hear our heavenly Father speak to us, with the laughter of grace in his voice, saying, "I love you. In my Son, I've walked the path before you. Seek me with all your heart, and you will find me. The privilege of knowing me is available to everyone, regardless of the blessings or heartaches that your family on earth has brought to your life."

One friend felt jealous as he read this book; he doesn't have five generations of Christian heritage. The sheer mystery of unequally distributed blessing can be enraging. But even more, as my friend remarked, mystery points up the sovereign wisdom of God who writes each of our stories so differently, but always with the intention of preparing us for our part in his story. The mystery of his plan, when seen as a reflection of inscrutable goodness, leaves us not only rejoicing with others more blessed, and confused by choices he never explains, but also awed by the love behind the plan that one day will have us all singing. ❧

Reflections of Two Sons and Grandsons:

The God of Our Father and Our Grandfather

❧

Reflections of Kep Crabb

My name is Kep, and I'm Larry, Jr.'s, firstborn, twenty-five-year-old son. Six months ago, Dad sent me a copy of the manuscript for this book and asked me to reflect on how this record of two generations of family history touches me.

Most of you are hearing these stories for the first time. I've heard most of them before. But I've never heard them told in one sitting. Reading them in one book has given me an understanding of a disturbing fact that never before hit me quite so clearly: life offers no guarantees, at least not the ones I may want.

I have lots of questions about that. What will my life be like? Will people I love die, as happened to my grandfather and my dad? Will my life be a struggle?

What does God have planned for my life? Who can assure me of anything as I face the rest of my life?

Reading Grandpa's stories about his life—the tragedies, the blessings, his struggles with severely tested faith—was richly meaningful. I felt hope in a world that sometimes feels hopeless. It struck me that everyone will feel the cruel sting of life. God is not a terribly safe person to trust, but somehow it all makes sense.

Many of us will not be asked to overcome the hardships that my grandfather endured; some will be asked to overcome far more. The one sure thing is that all of us, at some point, will have our faith challenged.

As I anticipate whatever may lie ahead for me, I feel especially thankful for the unique blessing of growing up around people who genuinely love the Lord. Not too many people in my generation have been similarly blessed. Memories of events that felt warm when they happened now feel not only warm but also sustaining.

Even though I'm young, it seems like so long ago when Mom, Dad, Ken, and I pulled up the long dirt driveway of my grandparent's South Carolina home. We were greeted by a plate of Grandma's freshly baked cinnamon rolls and Grandpa's laugh. This book may not have let you hear Grandpa's laugh, but I want you to know he laughs well; he laughed well when he was a child, and he laughs well now. He loves to be on either the telling or listening end of a good joke. He enjoys life, even though his rich blessings have been mixed with heart-breaking tragedies. I always marvel that he has come through all his painful experiences with the ability to have a really good time. Not many people could have experienced his life and come through it with a positive attitude, let alone a sense of humor. It strikes me that he is not bitter or resentful about the tough things life has brought him. I pray that one day I will look back over my life, with whatever hardships come my way, and be able to laugh as Grandpa does.

Maybe his laughter comes out of his understanding of serious things. I've often heard him talk about the larger story that God is telling through his life. He believes that his heavenly Father is totally controlling not only the larger story but also Grandpa's part in it. Grandpa's life is rooted in that belief.

I see no other explanation for how a man can make it after as a five-year-old watching his father die, watching his brother die without making clear his faith in Christ, and hearing over the phone that his son had been killed in a plane crash. That's a lot. How did he make it through those hard experiences and still be able to laugh?

For reasons I can't fully grasp, my grandfather really believes that God is good, and he trusts him enough to depend on his grace. Belief and trust. That may seem like such a pat answer. But believing and trusting don't come easily. Sometimes trust comes after screaming at God. Sometimes belief and trust are the hardest decisions for us to make.

I write all this from the perspective of someone whose life so far has been almost a fairy tale. My tough times haven't severely tested my faith. I grew up in a comfortable home with parents who love me. I'm about to marry the woman of my dreams. In the things that matter, life couldn't be better. But this book reminds me that trials will come. While that's not a happy thought, I would like to think that in at least some ways I'm ready and willing to face them. My grandfather allowed difficulties to draw him closer to God and become more dependent on him. That's what I want too (James 1:2–4; 1 Peter 1:6–8).

Until then, I'll enjoy my blessings, including parents who train others in marital relating and parenting. If Dad ever writes a book about raising children, I'm sure he'll title it *By the Seat of My Pants*. He has told me that whatever formulas he earlier thought would work were thrown out as he struggled to deal with me. I was no easy assignment.

But my parents never gave up. They never quit praying for me, loving me, even when it would have been far easier to love me less.

When I think about my father, I think of the time we went shopping together at K-Mart. I was about six years old at the time. As we drove to the store, I asked him if I could buy a toy. He said I could, but he put a limit on the amount of money I could spend from my allowance.

A special toy rifle caught my eye. It cost more than the amount my dad said I could spend, but I bought it anyway.

As Dad and I met at the door and began walking toward the car, he noticed my package. He looked at the contents and asked me how much it had cost. After I muttered an amount he couldn't hear, he made me tell him the price. He turned around, pulling me with him, and told me to return the gun.

I had disobeyed him; that was a serious matter. I was scared to death. I went to the return counter and waited in a line of customers for about ten minutes, all the while terrified that I was about to be spanked.

When I had exchanged the gun for my money, I slowly walked to the door where Dad was waiting. I didn't notice the package he was carrying as we crossed the parking lot to our car. When we got in, he handed it to me and told me to open it. It was a gun, identical to the one I had just returned.

"That's for you," he said and smiled.

I looked at him with confusion written all over my face. "Why are you giving this to me? I thought you would spank me."

"You deserve to be spanked because you disobeyed me," he said. "But I'm giving you a gift instead. That's what God does when we admit to him that we've been wrong.

"Our heavenly Father," he continued, "forgives all our sins if we believe that Jesus took the spanking we deserve."

I didn't become a Christian then, but my dad planted the seed of the gospel in me that day, and that seed bore fruit years later. That day my father demonstrated what he knew of his Father's mercy and grace.

Reading about the God of my father and the God of his father provoked two strong reactions in me. First, I have an even deeper respect for my grandfather. As he walked his path in life, he let God lead him through it all to a deeper faith. I'm thankful that God has given me a chance to know my grandfather, a privilege not everyone has.

Second, something I've been hearing most of my life is beginning to make more sense: God really is good. This truth is often hard to believe. But the lives of my grandfather and my father bear testimony that it's true.

I sincerely hope that *God of My Father* encourages you to walk the path toward God. That's what it has done for me.

Thanks, Grandpa and Dad, for opening your hearts. I've learned that the one absolute guarantee we have is the only one we really need: God is moving through every detail of my life to make me like his Son. And because his Son died for my sins, the God of my grandfather and the God of my father is waiting for me to be with him through all eternity.

Reflections of Ken Crabb

When my father first asked me to read the manuscript of this book and write down my reflections, I was mildly interested. But after reading the book, my mild interest turned to excitement. I found myself wanting to express in words my reaction to this intensely emotional book. Some chapters touched me deeply; others spoke of things that are simply beyond me.

I have never experienced the death of someone as close as a father. When my uncle Bill died, I grieved more for my aunt, grandparents, cousins, and father than for myself. In my twenty-two years, I have yet to experience such a faith-testing loss. I know my time will come, and I only hope and pray that I will respond the way Grandpa responded to tragedy in his life. He endured deep pain and troubling doubt, but he always returned to the path that leads to God. That's the path I want to walk too.

In some ways, Grandpa's childhood was very different from mine. He was raised with neither a father nor a generous supply of money. Although I have spoken to others about Grandpa's rough childhood, I never realized until I read this book about the significant resources God provided to help him. He was blessed with an incredibly godly and loving mother. I look forward to meeting her. He also had powerful memories of a really good father. Both of his parents were committed to the Lord and to their family. Although Grandpa lacked what most people in my generation regard as necessary advantages, Grandpa was better off than many of my friends are today.

I believe that one of the greatest gifts my wife, Carolyn, and I can give to our yet-to-be-born children is what my great-grandparents gave to my grandfather, what my grandparents gave to my parents, and what our parents gave to us: a love for the God of their fathers, a love for each other, and a love for their children.

Grandpa's reactions to his early adulthood have made me think of my present situation and attitudes. Too often I *tell* God where I am heading. I'm a terrific planner. I have organized the rest of my life in clear detail, year by year. I know how many kids I want, their gender and abilities. I have charted my career up through my retirement. I just hope that God agrees with my plan.

Grandpa talks about turning over the captain's post to Christ and following where he leads. This is one of my greatest struggles. I want to grow in Christ, but I'm frankly reluctant to ask God to do whatever it takes to bring me closer to him. He just might ruin my plans. I find myself still stubbornly resisting turning over the wheel. I think I'm too scared to ask God for the maturity to let go.

Grandpa's passion for the church is so strong that he had a hard time dealing with differences in the church. Carolyn and I have recently found a church we enjoy attending. We like the music, and we both are nurtured and instructed by the preaching. But I wish I had Grandpa's deep love for worship. My Sunday morning can easily be ruined by one angry exchange with Carolyn on the way to church. For months I've been praying for the ability to clear my mind and really worship for one hour. I'm batting about .500. Obviously I have a long way to go.

My dad also struggles with differences he and his dad have had over the years. And yet they have come to the place where they can disagree with each other without disrespecting each other. I'm growing in that area with Dad. Because he and I have similar struggles, I value him as my mentor. And within the last few years, I have developed the courage (not always the wisdom) to disagree with him. I love to stand firm on *my* convictions.

I guess I also still struggle to win my father's blessing and respect, even though in most ways he has already given it to me. Yet I find myself reading the Bible to find support for my position rather than to let God teach me. I suspect I'm still trying to impress my dad with what I know.

When I think about my grandfather's and father's struggles with God's predictability and goodness, I realize that from my present perspective, God seems predictably good. I realize that predictability and goodness are two different things that, especially in God, don't always go together. In fact, they rarely do.

God has blessed my life with two wonderful parents, a brother who is also a close friend, a terrific wife from a family similar to mine, and several really good friends. Recently God added to my list of blessings a job that I love, the exact job I wanted since I was a junior in college. For me to be angry with God seems comparable to a five-year-old getting mad at Santa Claus after an overly generous Christmas morning. I really can't imagine many good things that God hasn't already given to me.

What have I done to deserve all that I have? What have I done to be so blessed? I think I know the answer: nothing! And I also know that I have no guarantee of things continuing so comfortably.

I don't look forward to the desert times that lie ahead. But, although I try to prepare myself for the hard times and foolishly attempt to plan carefully enough to avoid them, I know that at my core I want to know God as my father and his father do. I would just like to get there by an easier route than they've taken.

Thinking about my grandparents dating is a fun thought. Most younger people can't imagine their parents, let alone their grandparents, as two kids dating. But I can picture both my mother and dad *and* Grandma and Grandpa dating because after twenty-

seven and fifty-five years of marriage, the signs of courting are still there in each relationship. I like that.

Our marriage, after thirteen months, is good, but I
long for the kind of intimacy I see in my parents and
grandparents. I believe Carolyn and I are in the earliest
stages of being *in love, in Christ, in God* as Grandpa
described. But I realize too that an immature version of
being "in love" must give way to something richer. In
Mere Christianity, C. S. Lewis wrote, "Being 'in love' is
compared to loving as a dog paddle is to swimming."
Splashing around is fun, but I can't wait to swim like an
Olympian. I love Carolyn. We're committed to each
other for life; divorce is not an option. But I want something more. I want for both of us the depth of closeness
that my parents and grandparents visibly have in their
marriages.

Grandpa has given much thought to whether or
not people will miss him when he dies. I don't think
about that very much. I suppose I'm just too young.
Maturity may lead me to ask many questions that don't
occur to me now. Reading Grandpa's thoughts made me
recall a conversation I had with Grandpa in my parents'
kitchen. I mentioned a movie I had seen with some
friends. Without a mood of condemning me, Grandpa
said that movies seemed so trivial to him now. He went
on to comment how many things of this world have lost
their appeal and how thoughts of heaven consume his
mind.

This conversation made it clear, if ever I had any
doubt, that this eighty-year-old and twenty-two-year-
old were on opposite sides of a yawning canyon. I can't
begin to imagine heaven with the intense clarity I sense
in Grandpa when he speaks of it. It discourages me to

realize that the bridge I must build to reach the side he stands on will require a construction process I can't plan. I assume that the bridge will be built by wrestling with a series of unexpected difficulties that will leave me with nothing but God. My left-brained rationality is tormented by the prospect of feeling mysterious passions and levels of pain I have not yet known. But I am confident they will reflect the work of a good God who is completing his work in me before I go to be with him.

Grandpa has experienced life from the perspective of three generations—as a son, father, and grandfather. Dad knows two of these. Because I'm in the beginning stages of adulthood, I know only one.

Reflecting on my few years, I'm thankful for the many blessings. But through writing this book, Dad and Grandpa have helped me see that the best is yet to come. I have the rare privilege of watching my father and my grandfather walk ahead of me, nearly thirty and sixty years ahead, on a path that I want to walk with them when I'm in their stages of life.

As I read *God of My Father*, it struck me that Grandpa has lived a very full life. He has walked through many fires, and although he has been singed, he did not burn. Rather, he emerged with a tested faith that has made him strong. That strength is evident. I can see it.

Dad also has been through trying times. And he too remains faithful. As I read Dad's letter to Kep and me, I cried a lot. The letter made clear how strongly he desires for us to know God. It made me feel both humbled and drawn.

Even more humbling and drawing is the realization that his desire is infinitely less than God's passionate longing to reveal himself to me. I think I have some idea how much my father loves me. I'll never forget the letter I received from him while I was in college and he was on sabbatical in England. The letter simply said, "Just thought you should know I'm thinking about you and praying for you. I love you. Dad." No advice. No news. Just an expression of love. I felt it.

But Dad's love is only a reflection of the love my heavenly Father feels toward me. I'm grateful that I've felt it through my earthly father. In the center of my being, my only desire is to know the God of my father and the God of my grandfather. With their example leading the way, I know the best is yet to come.

DISCUSSION GUIDE

This is a deeply personal book. It gives a glimpse into my father's "midnight ramblings," where he expresses his fears and doubts, passions and joys. It lets you hear my responses to what for me has been the clearest glimpse into Dad's passions. And it lets you look at my sons coming up the path behind us.

I said in the book's introduction that this is a book about mentoring: how an older person influences a younger person for good. Each of us has been affected by mentors: teachers, bosses, parents, pastors, or colleagues. Each of us has spiritual mentors: people who have drawn us to deeper faith in God. My spiritual mentor is my father. In some ways, that means this a book about father-son relationships as well.

The goal of the questions in this discussion guide is to help you do three things:

1. reflect on and appreciate the mentors in your life;

2. become a more conscious mentor to the people walking behind you on the path;

3. explore some of the personal feelings and issues this book raises.

Use the discussion questions to fit your particular situation. Many of you will not name your father as your spiritual mentor; others of you will discover that your father was more of a mentor to you than you realized. Some of you, like my dad, grew up without fathers, either because they had died or because they were physically or emotionally absent. Don't let that prevent you from exploring how other people have helped shape you. If a question isn't appropriate for your relationship to your father, use it to reflect on your relationship to another mentor in your life.

Although this guide is written primarily for men to use, I encourage women also to use this book and study guide to explore how people have mentored them in significant ways. Please don't be distracted by my use of male examples and masculine pronouns. Look beyond that to the dynamic between mentor and learner, parent and child. The same is true for unmarried readers. When Dad reflects on his marriage and his love for my mother, I suggest you ask questions about your parents' marriage and your own marriage. However, if you are not married or if you were raised by a single parent, don't let these questions exclude you. Think of a marriage that has had a positive impact on you. Then try to respond to the discussion questions with that marriage in mind.

Most of the questions in this discussion guide can be used in group settings, allowing people to share their stories, to listen and learn from each other. Some questions are more appropriate for personal reflection and can best be answered in a journal. In fact, I recommend keeping a journal of your responses to these questions; it will deepen your experience of exploring the God of your father, of understanding how God has used other people to shape you, and of understanding how he is using you to shape other people.

However you choose to use this discussion guide, I pray that it will help you to see not only the legacy your father/mentor left you but also the ways you can be a mentor to your children or other young people. Share your life and your stories with them. Tell them your joys, your questions, and your passions. Share your faith with them.

Definition of a Father

1. How would you define the path you are following? In what ways do you want your children to walk the same path? In what ways does your walk on the path attract your children to want to follow you?

2. What is life like for your children? What do you want their lives to be like?

3. Are your children more important than anything else in your life? Explain. What would your children say is the most important thing in your life?

Introduction

1. I was deeply affected by my father's journal because in it I was hearing his story. Have you heard your father's story—his experiences and perceptions of his life? In what ways has that story shaped you?

2. The Introduction states that mentoring is "how an older person influences a younger person for good." In what ways has your father been a mentor to you? In what ways have you followed the path he has walked? What made that path attractive to you?

3. If your father has not been your primary mentor, who has played that role? In what ways have you followed the path your mentor has walked? What made that path attractive to you?

4. Are you a mentor to your children or to younger people you know? In what ways have your children followed you on the path? What do you do to make that path attractive for your children? How are you sharing your story with them?

5. In what ways does your father/mentor draw you to love God? Do you reveal God to your children or distort and obscure him? Explain.

6. The Introduction states, "Everyone's life is a story whose point is discovered only when that story is lifted up into the larger story of God." How is this statement true of your father/mentor's story? How is it true of your story?

Chapter 1:
Hush! God Is in It

A Father's Recollection . . .

1. As my father describes his childhood home, we get a glimpse of his family's character. What physical things about your childhood home reveal positive qualities of your parents?

2. How did you perceive your father when you were five years old? Did you eagerly await his arrival home, as my dad did, or did you dread his arrival, as his friend Manuel did? Explain.

3. What did you learn about the character of God from watching your father interact with your mother?

4. My grandfather's death when Dad was only five years old created great confusion in him. It shook his idea of who God is: "God let my papa die." What childhood experiences made you question God's character? Have you recovered from the trauma? What or who helped you get through the crisis?

5. My dad lived most of his life without a father; yet his story reveals his father's deep influence on his life. In many ways, the five-word phrase, "Hush!

God is in it," was my grandfather's legacy to him.
The power of those words continued to comfort
my dad and anchor his faith long after his father's
death. What legacy has your father left you? How
has it anchored your faith?

6. As Dad grew into manhood, he chose to cherish
what his father's death *gave* him rather than complain about what that death *robbed* from him. If
your father's death—or his life—has robbed you of
knowing a loving father, what can you choose to
cherish about him?

7. My dad's statement, "I know that in all that happens, God has a master plan" is a statement of deep
faith because of the sorrow and loss he experienced. In what ways can you affirm this statement
of faith? What agonizing experiences have given
depth to your ability to believe this?

8. My father accepted that we will never understand
God's ways, but we will know "enough of his character to rest." What characteristics of God help you
to rest in the midst of confusing circumstances?

A Son's Reflections . . .

9. As I reflect on my grandfather's dying words, I
wonder whether his faith, which affirmed that God
was in everything, was mature or naïve. I decide it
is mature because it became the compass that kept
my father on the path toward God. In what ways
has the faith of your father/mentor been a compass
for you, keeping you on the path toward God?

10. Comment on the question: "How can I hush, knowing only that God will be in whatever happens?" Do you ever feel like this? How do you resolve this inner tension?

11. Is it easy or hard for you to trust God in the midst of tragedy or uncertainty? What makes it easy or hard for you? In what ways has your father/mentor helped you trust God in these circumstances?

ॐ

Chapter 2:
It's Our Last Nickel, Lawrence.
Don't Lose It

A Father's Recollection . . .

1. My father's childhood family had very little. Sometimes they were down to their last nickel. Yet he says of his mother, "Mother gave thanks, as always." She modeled a trust in God's unfailing care. What qualities of faith did your parents/mentors model for you? What qualities of faith are you modeling for your children?

2. When my dad and his brother earned money, they gave it to their mother. What little they had, they shared. In what ways did your childhood family practice this kind of cooperation, interdependence, and sharing? In what ways has our society lost these qualities?

3. My dad recognizes that his mother taught him to pray, not only by her example of praying but also by spending time listening to each of her children pray each night. Who taught you to pray? How did that person teach you? In what ways are you teaching your children to pray?

4. Even as a young child, my father realized that his family was rich in the things that mattered: love,

time, attention, trust, faith, togetherness. He tells of the wealthy parents who were too "important" and "busy" to be involved with their children. Which of these two family dynamics characterizes your childhood home? How would your children describe their family atmosphere?

5.　Dad looks back on a Christmas morning and sees with adult eyes the selfless love his mother expressed in giving her children gifts. Using your adult eyes, think back on your own childhood and pinpoint one or two interactions that reveal characteristics you hadn't realized before in your parents.

A Son's Reflections . . .

6.　What is your response to the statement, "Hardship draws out of us something good and strong and noble, qualities that sometimes develop in no other way"? On what personal experiences do you base your response?

7.　In what ways have shared trials drawn you together with other people in Christ? In what ways have shared trials brought your family together in Christ?

8.　My father taught me about transcendence: that beyond my life exists a story that is bigger than mine. If you understand the idea of transcendence, who taught it to you? In what ways did that person reveal to you the bigger story? What are you teaching your children about the bigger picture?

9. How do you respond to the statement, "I've received no greater gift from both my parents than the realization that I was not then and am not now the most important person in their lives"? Were you the most important person in your parents' lives? How do you feel about that? Who was the most important person in their lives?

10. I believe that "only when we love God more than family do we free our spouses and sons and daughters to become preoccupied with Someone greater than themselves." In what ways do you agree or disagree? If you agree, how are you living that out in your own family? Who would your children say is the most important person in your life?

Chapter 3:
Having Nothing, Yet Possessing
All Things

A Father's Recollection . . .

1. Dad recalls Mrs. Bell "bullying" him into a conversion. Have you or your children ever had an experience like that? How did that experience affect your spiritual development?

2. God used a warm-hearted evangelist to mentor my father and draw him to faith. What non-family people has God used to draw you to himself? What characteristics of those people attracted you? How did they mentor you?

3. My dad remembers that Harold Harper cared for him and encouraged him. In what ways are you caring for and encouraging younger people to walk the path toward God?

4. "Mother wrested comfort from the most impossible circumstances," Dad says of his mother. He realizes the strong impact her example had on her children. What examples of godliness have your parents set for you? In what specific ways have those examples shaped your life?

5. Even though my dad's family was poor, the chil-
    dren did not feel deprived. What was the source of
    their contentment?

6. What was your childhood family's view of prosper-
    ity? In what ways was your family wealthy? How do
    you and your children define "having everything"?

A Son's Reflections . . .

7. What "innocent joy" do you remember from child-
    hood? In what ways has that innocent joy changed
    over the years?

8. What is your response to the statement, "For years,
    I tried to convince myself that my life might never
    be touched by serious tragedy, that my soul could
    find satisfaction and rest in what Christians like to
    call the blessings of life"?

9. Do you believe that "tragedy is an undercurrent in
    everyone's life, with occasional eruptions that
    come with neither warning nor explanation"? What
    circumstances have led you to that belief? What
    personal tragedies have you faced? In what ways
    does your Christian faith impact that belief?

10. How do your children see you responding to
    tragedy? What beliefs are you expressing to them?

11. I have come to believe that God is good, even
    when tragedy strikes. That becomes a new "basis of
    joy, a mature joy that has lost the innocence of
    Eden but gained the security of hope." Do you
    affirm that belief? Where are you on the journey

from the innocence of Eden to the security of hope?

12. As I think about my grandmother, I realize she valued the *usefulness* of her life more than the *quality* of her life. What people in your experience have modeled that same value? How did they express it?

13. Hearing Dad describe his mother makes me think about my mother. I described her as a behind-the-scenes woman whose tenderness and passion are more easily expressed through deeds than words. "Mother is more concerned with *loving* than with *saying*, 'I love you.'" What was your mother like? How did she communicate her love for you? How do you communicate your love to your children?

14. When my dad was young, people gave money to his mother so that his brother and sister could attend private schools. But Dad and his younger sister had to remain home and go to public schools. This situation would have made many children jealous and resentful. Instead, my dad turned "that painful reality into an avenue of blessing." What people in your life have turned their pain into avenues of blessing? What have you learned from their examples?

15. My father has helped me define masculinity realistically. "He can be insecure, and he fails, but he is not weak. He continues to move into his world in whatever way he believes God directs him." How do you define masculinity? What men have helped you define your masculinity?

16. In what ways are you modeling masculinity to other young men?

❧

Chapter 4:
I Made Only Ten Dollars Today

A Father's Recollection . . .

1. My dad longed for the security that a prosperous business would give him. Instead he had to learn to trust God on a day-to-day basis to provide for the necessities. What was the financial situation in your childhood home? What did you learn from how your parents handled financial security or insecurity? In what did they place their trust for security? How does that affect your life today?

2. Dad admits that although he thought he was praying for God's guidance in his business, he was merely asking for God's stamp of approval on his personal desires. In what areas of life is that true for you? What do you need to release completely to God's guidance?

3. My parents were a team, a "godly team doing his work in spite of crushing fatigue and discouraging finances." In what ways did your parents work as a team? In what forms of ministry were they involved? What do you find attractive about how they ministered, either individually or as a team? How has that affected your adult life?

4.   My father talks about alternating between "times of despair and times of firm confidence that God is good even when evidence of his goodness seems painfully lacking." Where are you in the spectrum between despair and firm confidence? How would other people say you are handling this time in your life?

5.   "I've tried to be the captain of my own ship," my dad confesses. "I want the Lord to be aboard with me. He is entirely welcome, as long as he stays out of the way as I direct. . . . As long as the sea remains calm, I feel as if I don't need him." In what ways have you tried to be the captain of your own ship? Where is the Lord on your ship?

6.   My dad came to believe that God is always helping us, even when we don't see him. Our part is to "turn over the captain's post to him and to follow wherever he leads, even when it is not where we want to go." What keeps you from turning over the captain's post to the Lord?

A Son's Reflections . . .

7.   As I watched my father's employees, I realized that his Christian faith and convictions had influenced their behavior and language. In what ways has your father's or your mentor's convictions influenced the people around him? In what ways do your convictions influence the people around you?

8.   When I made an adolescent, snobbish remark about one of my dad's employees, indicating that I

would never wear a blue collar, my dad reprimanded me: "Whatever you have, has been given to you. Never claim credit for it. Just use it well." He made me think about the worth of other people, the abilities God has given each of us, and my selfish pride. In what ways has your father/mentor helped you value other people and their abilities? In what ways do you see your abilities as a gift from God? How can you help your children put their abilities in a healthy perspective?

9. What is your response to the statement: "If our parents' primary effect on our souls has been good, we probably idealize them, more out of dependency and a need for them to continue feeding us than admiration. If their effect has been bad, we either inordinately idealize them to preserve a cherished illusion or harshly vilify them, seeing even their virtues as irremediably stained"?

10. I deeply respect my parents because they did not yield to discouragement. "They have not left the path of responsible Christian living to find relief from their problems." In what ways were your parents like or unlike my parents in this area? How does that affect your life now? In what ways are you tempted to leave the path of responsible Christian living to find relief? What effect will that have on your children?

11. I watched my father take his struggles to the Lord. Who has modeled that response in your life? In what specific ways has that person's example shaped you?

12. What is your response to the following statement? "The most profoundly good effect of a parent on a child does not come from consistent cheerfulness, self-confident strength, loving involvement, or generous material provision but from the parent's unrelenting pursuit of God, a pursuit that continues through every setback of life."

13. In what ways have you been encouraged to press on? In what ways have you determined to stay on the path even though your failures tempt you to quit?

❧

Chapter 5:
I Don't Want to Go
to Church This Morning

A Father's Recollection . . .

1. For my dad, church attendance was a conviction based on Scripture. What convictions about church life did your father/mentor hold? How have these convictions shaped your life?

2. The deep longing of my father's heart was to enjoy deep fellowship with other believers in the presence of Christ. What were your father's or mentor's deep longings about the church? Do you share that longing? If you do, how do you express your longing? If you don't agree, how do you handle your disagreement with your father/mentor?

3. A tension arose for Dad when his disagreement with the people in his church interfered with his desire for deep fellowship with them. In what ways has your father/mentor faced a similar tension? How did he handle it? What did you learn from watching him deal with this inner tension?

4. At the end of his vision, my dad says, "All those doctrinal positions I previously held as essential have not lost importance but are now seen in perspective. I realize that they are not worth causing

dissension and bitterness between those who truly
know and love our Savior. . . . Without relationship, which is the very center of Christianity, all our
doctrines are no more than sounding brass or tinkling cymbals." What is your response to his con-
clusions?

5. In what ways have you seen your father/mentor
    use his convictions as "pipes through which God
    pours out his love toward us"?

A Son's Reflections . . .

6. In what areas do you and your dad disagree? How
    do you handle your disagreements? How does your
    way of handling disagreement either hinder or
    enhance your relationship?

7. Are your children free to disagree with you? Do
    they *feel* they are free to disagree with you? Can
    they disagree respectfully? How does your way of
    handling disagreement with your children reveal
    God's character or point them to him?

8. My dad's convictions about church life matter to
    me. These convictions have sometimes made it
    hard for me to make my own decisions about
    church life. In what ways have you found that to be
    true in your relationship to your father/mentor?

9. When I make a decision I know my father would-
    n't make, I realize how much I long for his
    approval. In what ways do you long for your dad's
    approval? In what ways does that longing interfere
    with your ability to make decisions? If your father

is no longer living, how does your need for his approval still affect your life?

10. A son's desire for his father's approval results in a dynamic that gets in the way of productive mentoring. The first element of this dynamic is "the father's sense that his son has betrayed him when his son makes decisions the father would not make." Has your father/mentor felt betrayed when you make your own decisions? Have you felt betrayed when your children make decisions you wouldn't make? How has this betrayal, or lack of it, been expressed?

11. A second element of this dynamic is "a son's felt need to establish distance between himself and the man with whom he most wants to be close. . . . The son spends his life caught in the tension of wanting both independence and approval. To gain approval, he must cooperate with his father's view of life; but to feel independent, he must violate it." How has this dynamic worked in your relationship to your father/mentor and to your children?

12. As long as either my dad or I view our convictions as *poles* that keep us elevated above the other, our "efforts to influence the world will be felt as pressure that will either incite rebellion or promote compliance." But when our convictions become like *pipes* carrying God's love, our convictions will encourage dialogue and will invite others into deeper relationship. In what ways are your convictions like poles? In what ways can you change them into pipes carrying God's love and inviting people into deeper relationship? What specific change will you make in the next two weeks?

Chapter 6:
Let Me Be with
My Brother When He Dies

A Father's Recollection . . .

1. Dad recalls the good childhood memories he has of his brother, Cecil. What good childhood memories do you have of your siblings?

2. Deep discouragement plagued my dad because his only brother was not a Christian. Do you have siblings who are not Christians? How do you deal with that reality?

3. Dad saw his brother reveal many Christian virtues, even though Cecil chose to abandon his family's Christian faith. As a result, Dad said, "I resent Christians who speak of the wickedness of people who do not believe as they do." What did he mean? What people in your experience are like my dad's brother? How do you respond to them?

4. When my father prayed with his dying brother, he was aware that his words were not his own, that the Holy Spirit was praying for Cecil. Even though Dad has no way of knowing what went on in his brother's heart during or after that prayer, he takes comfort in knowing that the Spirit prayed for his brother. In what ways does this story comfort you?

5.   My dad's deep longing and prayer was to be with his brother when he died. "To speak of Christ as my big brother passed into eternity." When God said no to his plea and Cecil died, Dad struggled to believe in God's goodness. Describe similar struggles you have had.

6.   As my dad reflected on the funerals of his father, mother, and brother, he describes the contrast in the three events. In what ways have Christian funerals blessed you? What do you want your funeral to be like?

7.   In the end, my dad realized that his only strength came from the One who seemingly had disappointed him: "To whom else shall we go?" I see Dad's decision to trust God in that situation as an act of costly faith. It would have been easier for him to have stayed angry with God, to have erected barriers to his relationship to God. Instead, Dad chose to trust God's goodness even when he felt God had been cruel. In what ways has your father/mentor demonstrated a similar costly faith?

A Son's Reflections . . .

8.   Have you ever cried out, as I have, "God, I know you're good. But what good are you?" What situations prompted you to respond that way? Did you get stuck in that question, or were you able to move on? What or who helped you to move beyond your question?

9. It was hard for me to see my dad struggling both physically and personally without finding relief or a taste of God's presence. We pleaded with God to let my dad have some undisturbed sleep. But God did not answer our prayers with restful sleep. Instead, Dad slept even less and suffered more. I wanted to scream. When have you had a similar experience in your prayers for a family member? How did you handle it? What brought you out of the depths?

10. I was confronted with an enraging mystery. I believed God was able to help my father sleep, that he cared for him. But why wouldn't he act? What mysteries about God's character have you wrestled with lately? How have you handled the enraging mystery?

11. What is your response to the following realization? "I wanted to be confident that I could persuade God to do something; I was not willing to be confident in who God is, regardless of how he behaves."

12. Instead of answering my prayers for Dad's ability to sleep, Christ gave me a glimpse of himself. That glimpse helped me rest in the middle of unrelieved turmoil. Describe a time when God answered your cries with a glimpse of himself. What effect did this encounter with God have on your life?

13. "Perhaps the richest song is the expression of an unrelenting confidence in God's goodness even when we see absolutely no visible evidence to support it." In what ways are you able to sing the song? How are your children affected by your song?

🍂

Chapter 7:
I Screamed at God, But He
Wouldn't Repent

A Father's Recollection . . .

1. Have you watched your father/mentor respond to the death of someone close to him? What did you learn about your father/mentor? What did you learn about God?

2. How do you interpret my dad's screaming at God? Do you see it as a lack of faith?

3. Dad was painfully aware of how his response to death differed from his father's response: "Papa told us to hush in the presence of death. My immediate reaction was to scream." What is your response to the two mens' reactions?

4. In his letter to Bill, my father said he found comfort knowing that Bill was with the Lord and that life with Christ is far better than life on earth. What comforts you when you think about friends or family members who have died?

5. Dad speaks of God's "delightful unpredictability." What did that phrase mean to him? What does it mean to you?

6. The shared grief over their son's sudden death brought my parents together with an intensity they had never before experienced in over fifty years of marriage. "The wonder of those moments of closeness amidst the ashes of our son's death was truly a whiff of heaven." In what ways have you found richness in the midst of grief? In what ways have you had a "whiff of heaven"?

7. Discuss the differences in how my dad responded to his brother's death and his son's death. What accounts for the differences?

A Son's Reflections . . .

8. I am struck that my father's mind was "occupied less with missing Bill and more with the thought of Bill seeing Christ." Do you think his response was a denial of the reality of the deep loss, or do you think his joy was real? Have you watched a person react to death in a similar way? In what ways did that person's response shape you?

9. What is your response to the following statement? "If I had died, conversation about me would move . . . away from me and toward Christ. And that puts me in my place."

10. My dad's response to Bill's death revealed his perspective of parenting: "Make sure your kids know they're loved, but never put them in the place of God. That place can never be shared." Are your children in the right place? In what specific ways can

your love for God give your children security about their place in your life?

11. If my brother were able to speak to us, I think he would say that "God used my parents' refusal to back away from me to arouse my thirst for grace." How has God used your parents or your mentor to arouse your thirst for God? In what ways do you arouse your children's thirst for God?

12. Bill would say of our parents: "Their love for me outlasted the pain I caused them. They got mad at me, sometimes disgusted, but they never gave up." Who has shown that kind of love for you? In what ways did this person reveal that love? How have you been challenged to practice persevering love with your children? What will your children learn about God as a result of your patient love?

13. Bill would also say of our parents: "They are committed to Christ. . . . I knew that no matter what I did, they would keep on following Christ." Do your children know how deeply committed to Christ you are? How does your life reveal that? How does that commitment affect their lives?

14. In what ways did your father's life or your mentor's life reveal God's larger plan? In what ways does your life reveal to your children God's larger plan?

❧

Chapter 8:
I Wish I Could Tell Her How Much
I Love Her

A Father's Recollection . . .

1. How did your parents meet? What did you learn about your parents from hearing their story? Do your children know the story of how your parents met? Do your children know the story of how you and your spouse met?

2. My parents got married during a time of "grim economic realities," and their relationship was shaped by those realities. What difficulties did your parents face when they married? How did they handle those difficulties? How have those difficulties shaped their relationship?

3. "Ours would be a marriage of sharing: one bank account, no 'his' and 'her' distinctions." This is how my parents characterize their marriage. How would your parents characterize their relationship? How would you characterize your marriage?

4. My parents were very aware of God's purposes and expectations of marriage. What were your understandings of God's purposes and expectations of your relationship when you and your spouse

married each other? How has that understanding changed over the years?

5. My parents' marriage "survived misunderstand-ings, tears, and words spoken with the intent to hurt." Their commitment to each other was so strong that they always worked through their prob-lems, never contemplating separation or divorce as options. How did your parents handle their hurts and differences? How has that shaped your life? What is your commitment to your spouse?

6. "To be in love is to partake of the very essence of God," my parents believed. They saw God's love, expressed in Christ, as the only source of their love for each other. They believed they were "in love, in Christ, in God." How do you respond to this per-spective?

7. My parents believed that their marriage was a pic-ture of a larger story, of Christ's love for his church. Are you often aware that your marriage is a picture of the larger story? How does that perspective affect you? Who needs to see the picture of God's love through your marriage?

8. Christ set the pattern for marriage, a "pattern of other-centeredness, a radical, passionate commit-ment to devote all our resources to the welfare of the person we love." Whose marriage best illus-trates for you the passionate, other-centered com-mitment my parents describe? In what ways does your marriage reflect Christ's self-giving love? In what ways would you like to see your marriage grow?

A Son's Reflections . . .

9.   I'm aware of how difficult it is for both Dad and me to express our deepest feelings. In what ways are you like us? How have you worked to overcome this? What person in your experience is able to express his or her deep feelings appropriately? What can you learn from that person?

10. When I suggested that our family members might try to be more open with our feelings for each other, my dad responded, "The deepest bond between two people really can't be expressed in words." In what ways do you agree or disagree with his statement?

11. Do you believe there is a norm of openness toward which marriage partners should move? Explain.

12. What is your response to the following statement? "The couples whose level of intimacy seems enviable to me have been drawn together more often, I think, by profound kindness, shared hardships, and individual maturity than by courageous vulnerability or aggressive sharing."

13. In what ways do you express your *desires* to your spouse or best friend? How has that person responded? In what ways do you need to grow in your ability to express desires?

14. In what ways do you express *joy* to your spouse or best friend? How has that person responded? In what ways do you need to grow in your ability to express joy?

15. In what ways do you express your *struggle* to your spouse or best friend? How has that person responded? In what ways do you need to grow in your ability to express your struggle?

16. What are the "theme complaints" in your marriage or friendship? How have you handled them over the years?

17. Do you agree that not expressing our desires, joys, and struggles creates a barrier to intimacy? Explain.

18. "My father has taught me that the richest intimacy between a man and a woman grows out of something far more sublime than sharing feelings. The best marriage depends on a relationship with God through Christ, a relationship that frees us to love for a lifetime and to get better at it as we go along." In what specific areas or situations has God's love through Christ enabled you to love your spouse?

❧

Chapter 9:
Will I Be Missed?

A Father's Recollection . . .

1.   As my father reflects on people's response to his son's death, he wonders if people will miss him when he dies. Do you ever think about whether or not people will miss you when you die? Describe your thoughts.

2.   Dad says, "Oh, I know people will mourn [when I die]. But I want something more. Will I be missed as Bill is missed?" What is the "something more" he is looking for? What did Dad find attractive about people's response to Bill's life and death?

3.   Describing his grief over Bill's death, my dad says, "The richest sorrow is the kind I feel when I am alone with God and I talk to him about Bill. I find that missing Bill is a unique hurt that will never go away until I see him again." In what ways have you experienced a rich sorrow? How does Dad's sorrow express his love for Bill?

4.   In thinking about his own life, my dad realizes that people will miss him to the degree that they have seen Christ through his life. What people have revealed Christ to you through their lives? How did they reveal Christ? Through their behavior or char-

acter or words or convictions? In what ways are you revealing Christ to your children and to other people with whom you interact?

5. My dad longed to "make a difference in even one life." In some ways my dad's thoughts in this chapter reveal his humility. He doesn't think he has influenced the lives of very many people. Yet his family and friends know that he has consistently and clearly reflected Christ to us throughout his life. Have you made a difference in anyone's life? Make a list of people whom God in his grace has allowed you to touch. Were you aware at the time that you were mentoring these people? In what ways did Christ shine through your relationship? Take time to thank God for every situation in which he used your life to show himself to another person.

6. In the end, Dad realizes that his desire is not "to be missed when he dies" but to "walk close to the Lord, share his thinking, and become like him." In what ways does becoming more like the Lord prepare you to be an effective mentor? What can you do to walk more closely with the Lord?

A Son's Reflections . . .

7. Sometimes my father's life and questions leave me feeling insecure. I see the disappointments and difficulties he has experienced, and I ask, Will life be any different for me? Has your father or mentor left you with similar questions? Explain.

8.   I think I hear my dad saying to me, "Follow me as I have followed Christ. But get ready to be surprised. The path of pursuing God is very different from what you expect. At least it has been for me." What do you think your father's life or your mentor's life is saying to you? What is your life saying to the people who follow you on the path?

9.   Godly mentors disrupt the thinking of people who follow them on the path. My dad disrupted my thinking about several things. In what ways has your father or mentor disrupted your thinking?

10. While other people *tried to explain* God to me, my father *showed* me that God was an attractive mystery—too big to figure out but available enough to be known. What picture of God has your father or mentor given to you? What picture of God are you passing on to others?

11. Listening to my father pray when I was a child helped me to see God as a real person, someone I could talk to, someone who cared about me. What have your father's prayers or your mentor's prayers taught you about God? What have they revealed about that person's relationship to God? What do your prayers reveal about your relationship to God?

12. What is your response to the following statement? "Following Christ is a wild adventure full of risk, frustration, excitement, and setbacks."

13. As I follow my dad, I'm learning that the "path to God takes me beyond the classroom where I study his character and into the sanctuary where I enjoy

his heart." In what ways has your father/mentor led you along a similar path?

14. How do you define Christian maturity? Who, in your experience, exemplifies that maturity? By your definition, is your father/mentor a mature Christian? Are you a mature Christian?

15. I have come to realize that "perhaps maturity does not mean the end of struggle and failure so much as the courage to move through them." Do you agree or disagree? Explain. Using this definition of maturity, is your father/mentor mature? Are you mature?

ॐ

Chapter 10:
The Best Is Yet to Come

A Father's Recollection . . .

1. Although my father sometimes envied people who had no doubt, he came to realize that doubt is not the unpardonable sin, that God is not offended by our questions. How did your father handle doubt and questions when you were young? How has that helped or hindered your faith? How do you handle your children's questions?

2. When my dad thought about his papa's influence on his life and faith, he wrote him a letter, even though his papa has been dead for over seventy-five years. In this letter Dad told his papa that he had left good memories that have given my dad some "concept of the One we both call Father, even to the point that I affectionately call him Papa." Consider writing your father a letter explaining how he has helped you know and love God. If your father is living, consider mailing the letter to him. If he is not living or is inaccessible, use the letter, as my dad did, as an outlet. Or write letters expressing gratitude to some of the mentors who have shaped your life.

3. In thinking about his own death, my father wonders whether he will face death like Bunyan's Christian, who said, "I sink in deep waters; all his waves go over me. I shall not see the land" or like Hopeful, who said, "I see the gate, and those standing by to receive me." Who has given you a good model of facing death well? What attracted you about the person's perspective? How do you feel about your death?

4. Dad often speaks of catching a "whiff of heaven." And that whiff has made him long to be with the Lord and the members of his family who wait for him at the gate. For my father, the best is yet to come. Have you ever had a whiff of heaven? Explain. What makes you look forward to heaven?

A Son's Reflections . . .

5. As you reflect on your past, describe the legacy your parents, grandparents, and great-grandparents have left you. What particular characteristics of these people make you especially grateful?

6. In what way is the following statement true for you? "The effect of reflecting on my history, and especially on the God of my father, is to strengthen the conviction that my life is part of a larger story, a story that is continuing through me and on beyond me through my sons."

7. As you think of your part in the larger story God is telling, describe a particular personal experience that contributed to the "single purpose of dispel-

ling the fog with the dazzling sunshine of God's revealed character."

8. In what ways do you share my desire to see your children play their parts well in God's larger story?

9. Consider writing a letter to your children. If they are too young to understand, write a letter anyway and save it for them to read when they are older. In your letter tell your children what they mean to you and what your heart's desire is for them. Remind them of their heritage and that their lives are part of God's larger story. Challenge them to live for Christ.

10. How do you wish your children to "leave their mark" on the world? How can you free them to do that?

❧

REFLECTIONS OF TWO SONS AND GRANDSONS:
The God of Our Father and Our Grandfather

Kep Crabb's Reflections

1. Kep said that after reading my father's story, he "felt hope in a world that sometimes feels hopeless." In what ways was that your experience too? What particular parts of the story give you hope?

2. Kep is "thankful for the unique blessings of growing up around people who genuinely love the Lord." For Kep, these people also included his family. Think about the godly people whom God placed around you, both as you grew up and now. Who are the godly people God is placing around your children as they grow up?

3. One of the things that struck Kep about his grandfather was his ability to come through all his painful experiences with not only a positive attitude but also a well-developed sense of humor. Why do you think Kep finds this so attractive about his grandpa? What does this quality reveal to Kep about his grandpa's faith and perception of God? Who, in your experience, has modeled this quality for you?

4. Our sons have often heard their grandfather talk about the larger story that God is telling through his life. Have your children heard their grandparents tell their stories? How can you facilitate that? How can you create a setting that will allow your children to hear about their grandparents' struggles and joys and about their faith? If your parents are not Christians, how can you help your children see how their grandparents' lives were part of God's larger story, even though they did not entrust their lives to God?

5. Kep is attracted by two qualities he sees in his grandpa's life: belief and trust. What qualities do your children find attractive in their grandparents? What qualities in your parents would you like your children to recognize? How can you help that process?

6. In many ways my dad has mentored my sons: he has influenced them for good. Kep says, "My grandfather allowed difficulties to draw him closer to God and become more dependent on him. That's what I want too." In what ways have your parents mentored your children? How can you express your thanks to your parents for their influence?

7. I'm struck by the similarity in my brother's comments about our parents and Kep's comment about Rachael and me. They both said: *my parents never gave up on me.* I think those two comments reveal the power of mentoring. Rachael and I grew up seeing parents whose love for their children was

221

demonstrated in their refusal to give up when one of their children wandered from the path. Through those models, God has given us the grace to love our sons unconditionally. What threads of continuity do you see in the way your parents/mentors handled certain things and the way you handle the same kinds of situations?

8. Kep remembers a childhood incident that helped him see the character of God more clearly. What childhood experiences with your parents or grandparents gave you a glimpse of God's character?

9. In what ways have your grandparents' lives shaped you? If they are still living, consider writing them a letter expressing your thanks to them and describing how they have touched your life. Then take time to share with your children what impact your grandparents' lives have had on you.

Ken Crabb's Reflections

10. Although Ken has not yet experienced a "faith-testing loss," he has determined that when he does, he wants to respond the way his grandpa responded to tragedy in his life: "He endured deep pain and troubling doubt, but he always returned to the path that leads to God." What people, by their example of faith, are preparing you to face things that may lie ahead for you?

11. In what ways is Ken's statement about his grandfather also true of your grandparents or parents? "Although Grandpa lacked what most people in

my generation regard as necessary advantages, Grandpa was better off than many of my friends are today."

12. Ken says that one of the greatest gifts he and Carolyn want to give to their children is what their great-grandparents gave to their grandparents, what their grandparents gave to their parents, and what their parents gave to them: a love for the God of their fathers, a love for each other, and a love for their children. What are the greatest gifts your parents and grandparents have given to you? What are the greatest gifts you wish to give to your children?

13. Ken recognizes that his grandpa has struggled with many of the same issues he struggles with: giving over the control of his life to God, finding peace in the midst of uncertainty and chaos. What struggles do you have in common with your parents or your grandparents? What can you learn from how they have handled their struggles?

14. Ken also recognizes that his grandpa possesses a maturity that he can only imagine. Ken longs to love worship the way his grandpa does; he wonders if he'll ever anticipate heaven with the intensity his grandpa does. Which of your parents' or grandparents' qualities do you wish to have? How did they develop those qualities? What experiences in their lives helped shape those qualities?

15. Reflecting on the story of his grandparents' courting, Ken says, "Our marriage after thirteen months is good, but I long for the intimacy I see in my parents and my grandparents. . . . I want for

both of us the depth of closeness that my parents and grandparents visibly have in their marriages." Did your parents and grandparents give you positive models of intimacy and closeness? How did they communicate intimacy? If your parents did not model closeness, what marriage in your experience best exemplifies the closeness you would like to experience?

16. Aware of the "yawning canyon" that stands between where he is now in early adulthood and where his grandfather is, Ken says, "I assume that the bridge [to reach the side my grandpa now stands on] will be built by wrestling with a series of unexpected difficulties that will leave me with nothing but God." Do you agree? Explain.

17. Ken realizes that his parents' love for him has opened the way for him to begin to grasp God's infinite desire to draw Ken close to himself. In what way have your parents opened up the way for you to see God? How are you opening the way for your children to see and desire God?

18. I am deeply humbled and grateful to God that both of our sons see themselves on the path to God. I am grateful that my father has pointed the way both for me and for them. As you reflect on the influence your parents/mentors have had on you and the influence you are having on your children because of them, praise God for using families and mentors as an instrument in revealing himself and drawing us to him.